HMH

math expressions
Common Core

Dr. Karen C. Fuson

Watch the seahorse come alive in its underwater world as you discover and solve math challenges.

Download the *Math Worlds AR* app available on Android or iOS devices.

Grade **K**

Volume 2

This material is based upon work supported by the
National Science Foundation
under Grant Numbers
ESI-9816320, REC-9806020, and RED-935373.

Any opinions, findings, and conclusions, or recommendations expressed in this material
are those of the author and do not necessarily reflect the views of the National Science Foundation.

BIG IDEA 3 - Equations and Teen Numbers

BIG IDEA 4 - Equations for Partners

© Houghton Mifflin Harcourt Publishing Company

© Houghton Mifflin Harcourt Publishing Company

BIG IDEA 3 - More Teen Numbers and Partners

BIG IDEA 4 - More Story Problems and Equations

Student Resources

Dear Family:

Ask your child about our pretend grocery store at school! Children will be using the groceries from this pretend store to create addition and subtraction story problems, such as the following:

There are 3 bananas in this bunch and 4 bananas in the other bunch. How many bananas are there in all?

You and your child can create similar story problems with groceries in your own kitchen. When doing so, you may need to help your child say the question at the end of the story problem.

Addition example:
There are 5 cans on the top shelf. There are 4 cans on the bottom shelf. How many cans are there?

Subtraction example:
There are 10 eggs in the carton. If we cook 3 eggs, how many eggs are left in the carton?

It is not necessary to solve all of the story problems. Learning to visualize the situation and state the story problem are both important tasks, even without solving. Asking questions different ways is also helpful.

Have fun!

Sincerely,
Your child's teacher

Unit 4 addresses the following standards from the Common Core State Standards for Mathematics: **K.CC.A.1, K.CC.A.2, K.CC.A.3, K.CC.B.4, K.CC.B.4.a, K.CC.B.4.b, K.CC.B.4.c, K.CC.B.5, K.CC.C.6, K.CC.C.7, K.OA.A.1, K.OA.A.2, K.OA.A.3, K.OA.A.4, K.OA.A.5, K.NBT.A.1, K.MD.B.3, K.G.A.1, K.G.A.2, K.G.A.3, K.G.B.4, K.G.B.5, K.G.B.6, and all** Mathematical Practices.

Estimada familia:

¡Pregunte a su niño por la tiendita que tenemos en la escuela! Los niños van a usar los comestibles de la tiendita para crear problemas de suma y resta, como los siguientes:

Hay 3 plátanos en este racimo y 4 plátanos en el otro. ¿Cuántos plátanos hay en total?

Usted y su niño pueden formular problemas parecidos con los comestibles que tengan en su cocina. Al hacerlo, tal vez tenga que ayudar a su niño a formular la pregunta del final del problema.

Ejemplo de suma:
Hay 5 latas en el estante superior. Hay 4 latas en el estante inferior. ¿Cuántas latas hay?

Ejemplo de resta:
Hay 10 huevos en la caja. Si usamos 3 huevos, ¿cuántos huevos quedan en la caja?

No es necesario resolver todos los problemas. Aprender a visualizar la situación y a formular el problema son destrezas importantes, aun si los problemas no se resuelven. Formular preguntas de distintas maneras también es de mucha ayuda.

¡Que se diviertan!

Atentamente,
El maestro de su niño

CC SS En la Unidad 4 se aplican los siguientes estándares de los Estándares estatales comunes de matemáticas: **K.CC.A.1, K.CC.A.2, K.CC.A.3, K.CC.B.4, K.CC.B.4.a, K.CC.B.4.b, K.CC.B.4.c, K.CC.B.5, K.CC.C.6, K.CC.C.7, K.OA.A.1, K.OA.A.2, K.OA.A.3, K.OA.A.4, K.OA.A.5, K.NBT.A.1, K.MD.B.3, K.G.A.1, K.G.A.2, K.G.A.3, K.G.B.4, K.G.B.5, K.G.B.6** y todos los de Prácticas matemáticas.

cone

cylinder

corner

equation

cube

face

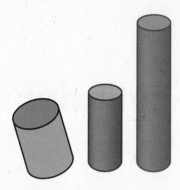

Examples:

$4 + 3 = 7 \qquad 7 = 4 + 3$

$9 - 5 = 4 \qquad 4 = 9 - 5$

 corner

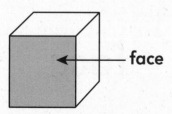 face

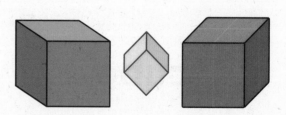

© Houghton Mifflin Harcourt Publishing Company

flat shapes	roll
greater than	solid shape
less than	sphere

© Houghton Mifflin Harcourt Publishing Company

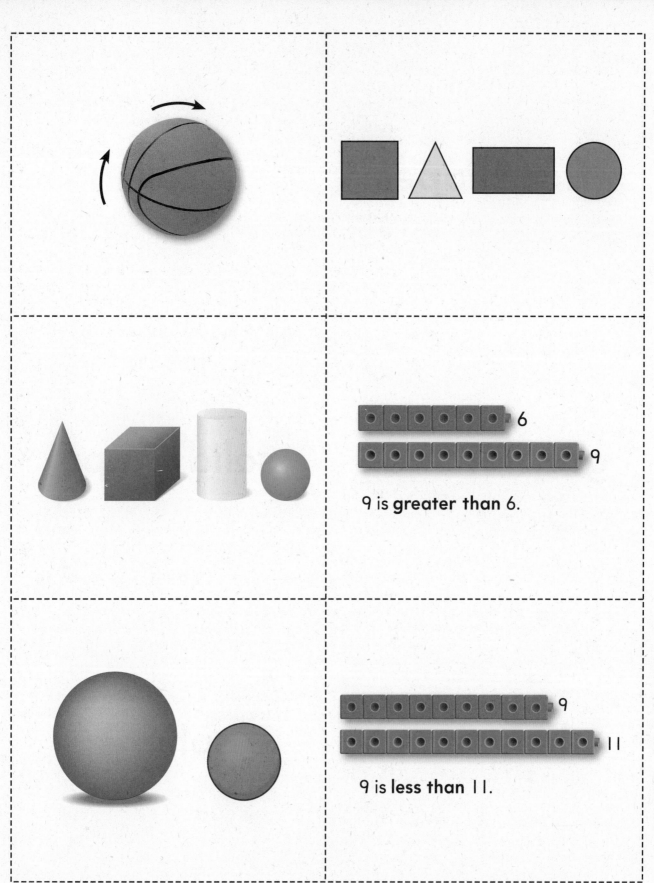

9 is **greater than** 6.

9 is **less than** 11.

stack

two-dimensional shapes

story problem

three-dimensional shapes

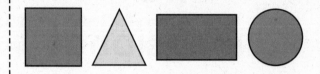

There are 2 bunnies in the garden.

Then 3 more bunnies come.

How many bunnies are there in total?

Name _____

Puzzled Penguin counted the cherries.

Look at what Puzzled Penguin wrote.

Help Puzzled Penguin.

14 cherries

Am I correct?

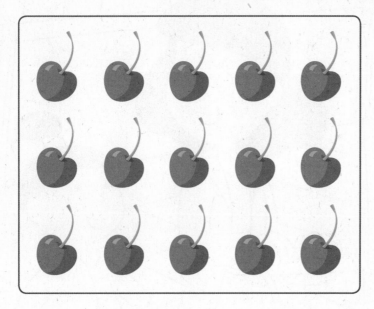

_____ cherries

✓ Check Understanding

TEACHER: Explain a way you can sort these fruits and vegetables.

Numbers 1–10 and Math Stories: Grocery Store Scenario

Cut on the dashed lines.

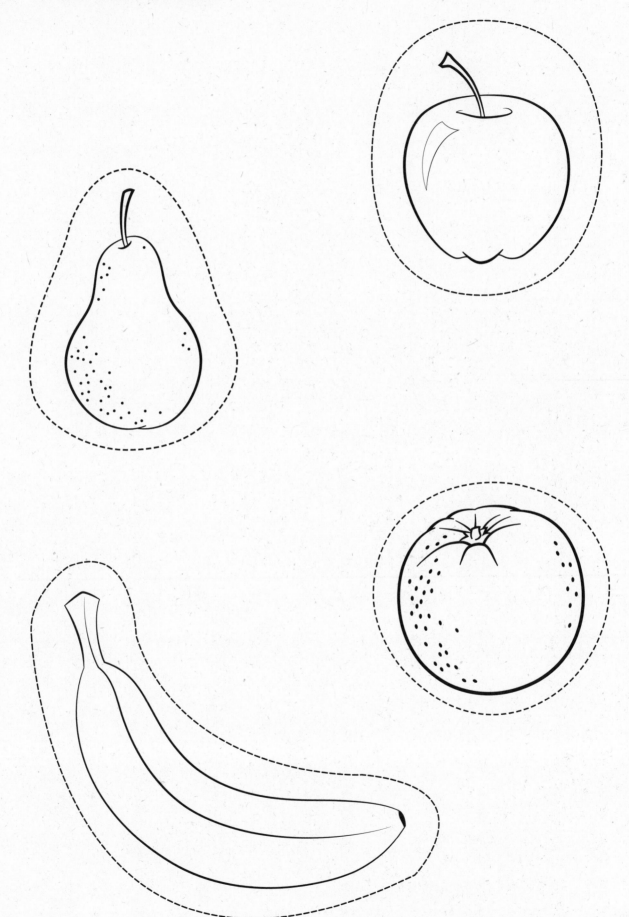

Fruit

Cut on the dashed lines.

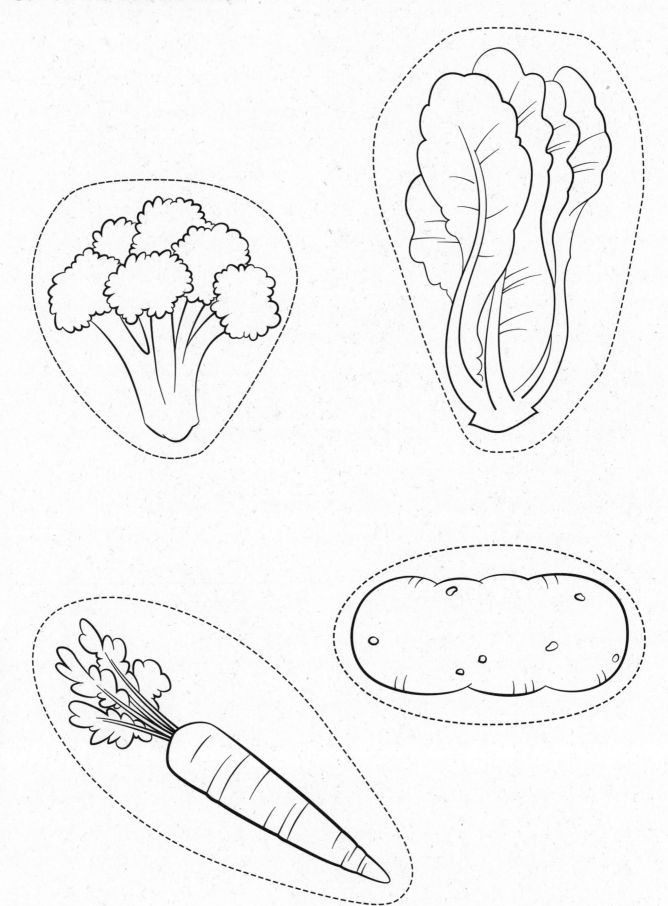

Vegetables **199**

Vegetables

Name _____

1 Draw a line to show the partners. Then write the partners.

   10 = ☐ + ☐

10 = ☐ + ☐

10 = ☐ + ☐

10 = ☐ + ☐

10 = ☐ + ☐

10 = ☐ + ☐

   10 = ☐ + ☐

   10 = ☐ + ☐

10 = ☐ + ☐

CCSS Content Standards **K.CC.A.3, K.CC.B.5, K.OA.A.1, K.OA.A.2, K.OA.A.3, K.OA.A.4**
Mathematical Practices **MP7**

2   Draw a line to show the partners. Then write the partners.
Begin with 9 + 1.

10 = ☐ + ☐

10 = ☐ + ☐

10 = ☐ + ☐

10 = ☐ + ☐

10 = ☐ + ☐

10 = ☐ + ☐

10 = ☐ + ☐

10 = ☐ + ☐

10 = ☐ + ☐

© Houghton Mifflin Harcourt Publishing Company

✓ Check Understanding

TEACHER: Draw objects to show partners for 7.

Find Partners of 10

Set A

$11 = 10 + 1$	$12 = 10 + 2$	$13 = 10 + 3$	$14 = 10 + 4$	$15 = 10 + 5$
$16 = 10 + 6$	$17 = 10 + 7$	$18 = 10 + 8$	$19 = 10 + 9$	$20 = 10 + 10$

Set B

$10 + 1 = 11$	$10 + 2 = 12$	$10 + 3 = 13$	$10 + 4 = 14$	$10 + 5 = 15$
$10 + 6 = 16$	$10 + 7 = 17$	$10 + 8 = 18$	$10 + 9 = 19$	$10 + 10 = 20$

Teen Equation Cards

Teen Equation Cards

Name _____

1 Show the partners with fingers. Then write the total.

$10 + 1 =$ ☐ $10 + 6 =$ ☐

$10 + 2 =$ ☐ $10 + 7 =$ ☐

$10 + 3 =$ ☐ $10 + 8 =$ ☐

$10 + 4 =$ ☐ $10 + 9 =$ ☐

$10 + 5 =$ ☐

2 Write the numbers 1–20.

3 Draw a picture to show 10 ones and 2 ones.

Content Standards K.CC.A.3, K.OA.A.1, K.OA.A.2, K.OA.A.3, K.OA.A.5, K.NBT.A.1
Mathematical Practices MP1, MP6

VOCABULARY
equation

4 PATH to FLUENCY Subtract the numbers. Use your fingers or draw.

$3 - 2 = \boxed{}$ $5 - 5 = \boxed{}$ $2 - 2 = \boxed{}$

$4 - 1 = \boxed{}$ $4 - 3 = \boxed{}$ $3 - 1 = \boxed{}$

$3 - 3 = \boxed{}$ $5 - 2 = \boxed{}$ $4 - 3 = \boxed{}$

$5 - 0 = \boxed{}$ $4 - 2 = \boxed{}$ $3 - 0 = \boxed{}$

$2 - 1 = \boxed{}$ $5 - 4 = \boxed{}$ $5 - 3 = \boxed{}$

5 Choose an **equation**. Draw a picture to show the subtraction. Write the equation.

 Check Understanding

TEACHER: Draw a way to show the number 17.

© Houghton Mifflin Harcourt Publishing Company

Name _____

1 Look at the partners. Complete the equations.

 $10 = \boxed{} + \boxed{}$

$10 = \boxed{} + \boxed{}$

$10 = \boxed{} + \boxed{}$

$10 = \boxed{} + \boxed{}$

$10 = \boxed{} + \boxed{}$

 $10 = \boxed{} + \boxed{}$

$10 = \boxed{} + \boxed{}$

 $10 = \boxed{} + \boxed{}$

$10 = \boxed{} + \boxed{}$

CC SS Content Standards **K.CC.A.3, K.CC.B.5, K.OA.A.1, K.OA.A.2, K.OA.A.3, K.OA.A.4**
Mathematical Practices **MP2**

Addition and Subtraction Stories: Grocery Store Scenario **207**

2 Look at the partners. Complete the equations.

 $10 = \boxed{} + \boxed{}$

$10 = \boxed{} + \boxed{}$

$10 = \boxed{} + \boxed{}$

 $10 = \boxed{} + \boxed{}$

$10 = \boxed{} + \boxed{}$

$10 = \boxed{} + \boxed{}$

 $10 = \boxed{} + \boxed{}$

 $10 = \boxed{} + \boxed{}$

 $10 = \boxed{} + \boxed{}$

✔ **Check Understanding**

TEACHER: Listen to this story, and solve. *Four children are sorting fruit for the grocery store display. One child leaves. How many children are still sorting fruit?*

$\boxed{}$ children

Addition and Subtraction Stories: Grocery Store Scenario

Name _____   Date _____

Add the numbers.

① $0 + 1 = \boxed{}$

② $1 + 2 = \boxed{}$

③ $1 + 3 = \boxed{}$

④ $2 + 0 = \boxed{}$

⑤ $3 + 2 = \boxed{}$

⑥ $4 + 1 = \boxed{}$

⑦ $1 + 1 = \boxed{}$

⑧ $2 + 2 = \boxed{}$

⑨ $0 + 3 = \boxed{}$

⑩ $2 + 1 = \boxed{}$

Name _____ Date _____

Subtract the numbers.

11. $1 - 1 =$ ☐

12. $2 - 1 =$ ☐

13. $4 - 2 =$ ☐

14. $5 - 2 =$ ☐

15. $3 - 2 =$ ☐

16. $4 - 3 =$ ☐

17. $2 - 0 =$ ☐

18. $5 - 1 =$ ☐

19. $4 - 1 =$ ☐

20. $5 - 5 =$ ☐

Dear Family:

Throughout the year, your child will be learning how to "break apart" numbers. For example, 6 equals 5 and 1, 4 and 2, and 3 and 3. We call two numbers that add up to a number the *partners* of the number.

To strengthen your child's understanding of these concepts, you can play *The Unknown Partner Game* with him or her. The game is played as follows:

Put out 5 objects such as buttons or crackers. Count them together. Have your child cover his or her eyes while you take a partner away. Ask your child to tell you the missing amount. Now it is your turn to close your eyes!

You can play this game again and again, starting with a different total each time. Start with 5 first (because it is easiest), and then move on to 6, 7, 8, 9, and 10.

Thank you!

Sincerely,
Your child's teacher

CC SS **Unit 4 addresses the following standards from the** Common Core State Standards for Mathematics: **K.CC.A.1, K.CC.A.2, K.CC.A.3, K.CC.B.4, K.CC.B.4.a, K.CC.B.4.b, K.CC.B.4.c, K.CC.B.5, K.CC.C.6, K.CC.C.7, K.OA.A.1, K.OA.A.2, K.OA.A.3, K.OA.A.4, K.OA.A.5, K.NBT.A.1, K.MD.B.3, K.G.A.1, K.G.A.2, K.G.A.3, K.G.B.4, K.G.B.5, K.G.B.6,** and all Mathematical Practices.

Estimada familia:

Durante todo el año su niño aprenderá a "separar" números. Por ejemplo, 6 es igual a 5 más 1, 4 más 2, y 3 más 3. A dos números que sumados dan como resultado otro número los llamamos *partes* del número.

Puede jugar al juego de las partes desconocidas con su niño para reforzar estas ideas. Se juega de esta manera:

Coloque en algún lugar 5 objetos, como botones o galletas. Cuéntenlos juntos. Pida a su niño que se tape los ojos mientras Ud. quita una parte. Pida a su niño que diga la cantidad que falta. ¡Ahora es su turno de cerrar los ojos!

Jueguen varias veces, siempre empezando con un total diferente. Empiecen con 5 (por ser el más fácil) y sigan con 6, 7, 8, 9 y 10.

¡Gracias!

Atentamente,
El maestro de su niño

CC SS En la Unidad 4 se aplican los siguientes estándares de los Estándares estatales comunes de matemáticas: **K.CC.A.1, K.CC.A.2, K.CC.A.3, K.CC.B.4, K.CC.B.4.a, K.CC.B.4.b, K.CC.B.4.c, K.CC.B.5, K.CC.C.6, K.CC.C.7, K.OA.A.1, K.OA.A.2, K.OA.A.3, K.OA.A.4, K.OA.A.5, K.NBT.A.1, K.MD.B.3, K.G.A.1, K.G.A.2, K.G.A.3, K.G.B.4, K.G.B.5, K.G.B.6** y todos los de Prácticas matemáticas.

Name _____

Color squares to show the number. Then complete the equation.

1 13

13 = _____ + _____

2 14

14 = _____ + _____

3 15

15 = _____ + _____

4 16

16 = _____ + _____

CC SS **Content Standards** K.CC.A.2, K.CC.A.3, K.CC.B.4, K.CC.B.4.c, K.CC.B.5, K.OA.A.1, K.OA.A.3, K.NBT.A.1 **Mathematical Practices MP3, MP6**

Practice with Teen Numbers and Partners **213**

Find the unknown partner. Draw squares to help you.

5   17

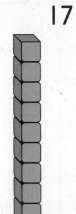

17 = _____ + _____

6   18

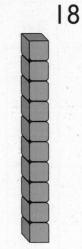

18 = _____ + _____

7   19

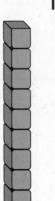

19 = _____ + _____

8   20

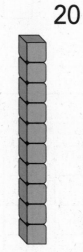

20 = _____ + _____

✔ ## Check Understanding

TEACHER: Complete the teen equation for 11.

11 = _____ + _____

Practice with Teen Numbers and Partners

Name _____

Draw lines to match. Ring the extras.

Write the numbers and compare them.

Write G for Greater and L for Less.

	5	G
	3	L

Count and write the number. Ring the number that is greater.

(3)   2

□   □

□   □

□   □

□   □

□   □

□   □

Count and write the number. Ring the number that is less.

□   □

□   □

□   □

□   □

□   □

□   □

Compare the numbers. Write G for **Greater than** or L for **Less than**.

2 L 3   5 ___ 2   4 ___ 5

✔ Check Understanding

TEACHER: Draw 2 groups of squares. Write how many in each. Ring the greater number.

Count, Match, and Compare

Name _____

Find the unknown partner. Draw squares to help you.

1

1 + ☐

2

2 + ☐

3

3 + ☐

4

4 + ☐

5

5 + ☐

Content Standards K.CC.B.5, K.OA.A.1, K.OA.A.2, K.OA.A.3
Mathematical Practices MP2, MP6

Practice Teen Numbers and Equations **217**

Find the unknown partner. Draw squares to help you.

6

7

1 + ☐

7

7

2 + ☐

8

7

3 + ☐

9

7

4 + ☐

10

7

5 + ☐

11

7

6 + ☐

© Houghton Mifflin Harcourt Publishing Company

✔ **Check Understanding**

TEACHER: Look at the equations. Explain why both ways of writing the equation are correct.

14 = 10 + 4   10 + 4 = 14

Practice Teen Numbers and Equations

Name _____

Draw a line to show two partners. Write the partners.

10 = ☐ + ☐   10 = ☐ + ☐

10 = ☐ + ☐   10 = ☐ + ☐

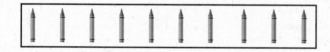

10 = ☐ + ☐   10 = ☐ + ☐

10 = ☐ + ☐   10 = ☐ + ☐

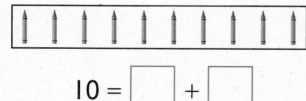

10 = ☐ + ☐

Content Standards K.CC.A.3, K.CC.B.5, K.OA.A.1, K.OA.A.2, K.OA.A.3, K.OA.A.4
Mathematical Practices MP3, MP6, MP7

Draw Tiny Tumblers on the Math Mountains.

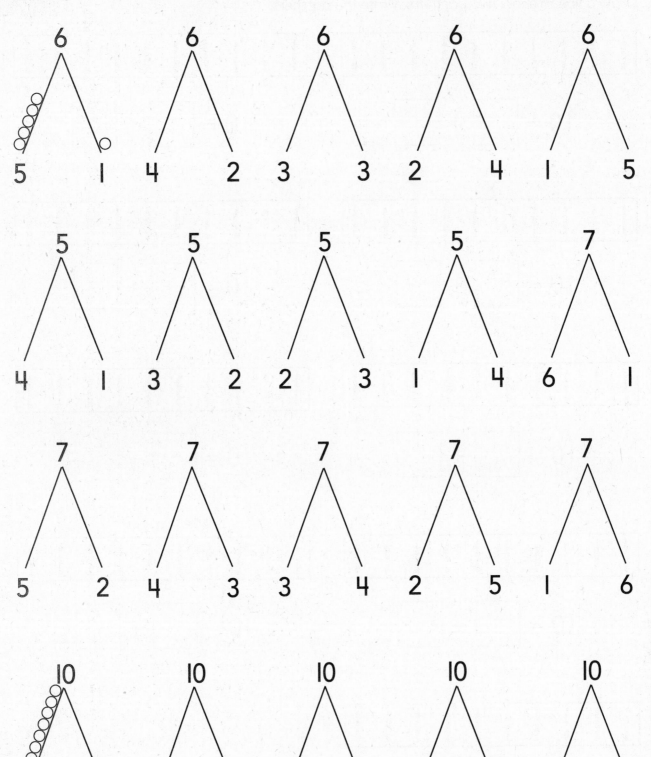

Break-Apart Numbers for 10

Name _____

Write the numbers 1 through 20 in order.

1									
									20

1									
									20

1									
									20

Count how many. Write the number.

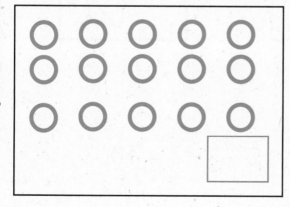

Break-Apart Numbers for 10 **221**

Write the numbers 1 through 20 in order.

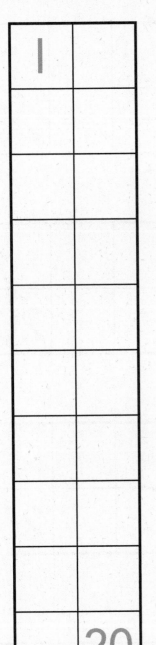

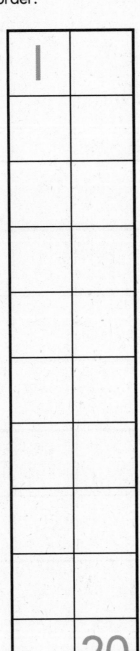

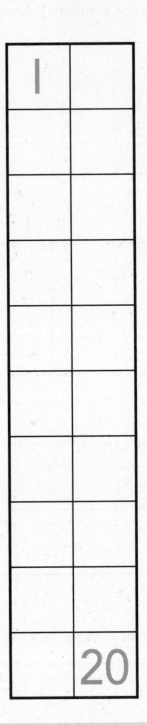

✓ Check Understanding

TEACHER: Fill in the unknown partner.

○○○○○○○○○○ (two filled circles followed by eight empty circles)

$2 + \boxed{} = 10$

Break-Apart Numbers for 10

Name _____ Date _____

Add the numbers.

1 $1 + 1 = $ ☐

2 $3 + 1 = $ ☐

3 $4 + 0 = $ ☐

4 $2 + 3 = $ ☐

5 $2 + 1 = $ ☐

6 $0 + 1 = $ ☐

7 $1 + 3 = $ ☐

8 $1 + 4 = $ ☐

9 $2 + 2 = $ ☐

10 $2 + 0 = $ ☐

Name _____ Date _____

Subtract the numbers.

⑪ $1 - 0 =$ ☐

⑫ $2 - 0 =$ ☐

⑬ $3 - 3 =$ ☐

⑭ $2 - 2 =$ ☐

⑮ $4 - 3 =$ ☐

⑯ $5 - 3 =$ ☐

⑰ $5 - 1 =$ ☐

⑱ $4 - 2 =$ ☐

⑲ $5 - 4 =$ ☐

⑳ $3 - 1 =$ ☐

Name _____

VOCABULARY
corner

1 Look at each shape. Write the number of straight sides.

---

2 Look at each shape. Write the number of **corners**.

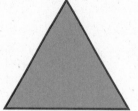

---

3 Ring the shape that has 4 sides of equal length.

4 Look at each shape. Ring the **flat shapes**. Mark an X on the **solid shapes**.

VOCABULARY
flat shapes
solid shapes

✔ Check Understanding

TEACHER: Explain the difference between these two shapes.

Attributes of 3-Dimensional Shapes

Name _____

1 Count and write the number. Ring the number that is greater.

(4) 2

2 Count and write the number. Ring the number that is less.

3 Write the numbers 1 through 20 in order.

CC SS Content Standards **K.CC.A.3, K.CC.B.6, K.CC.C.7**
Mathematical Practices **MP3, MP6**   Addition and Subtraction Drawings: Grocery Store Scenario **227**

4 Draw lines to match. Ring the extras. Write the numbers and compare them.
Write G for Greater than and L for Less than.

🍎🍎🍎🍎 (🍎🍎 ringed)	6	G
🍓🍓🍓🍓	4	L

🥕🥕🥕	☐	___
🍊🍊🍊🍊🍊	☐	___

🍓🍓🍓🍓	☐	___
🍌🍌🍌	☐	___

🍊🍊	☐	___
🌽🌽🌽🌽🌽	☐	___

🫑🫑🫑🫑🫑🫑	☐	___
🍇🍇🍇🍇🍇	☐	___

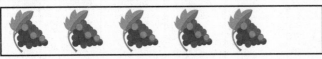

✓ **Check Understanding**

TEACHER: Look at the last exercise. Tell how you know whether 6 or 5 is greater.

Addition and Subtraction Drawings: Grocery Store Scenario

Name _____

1 Draw a line to show the partners. Write the partners.

10 = ☐ + ☐

10 = ☐ + ☐

10 = ☐ + ☐

10 = ☐ + ☐

10 = ☐ + ☐

10 = ☐ + ☐

10 = ☐ + ☐

10 = ☐ + ☐

10 = ☐ + ☐

Content Standards K.CC.A.3, K.CC.B.5, K.OA.A.1, K.OA.A.3, K.OA.A.4
Mathematical Practices MP3, MP6, MP7

2 Draw Tiny Tumblers on the Math Mountains.

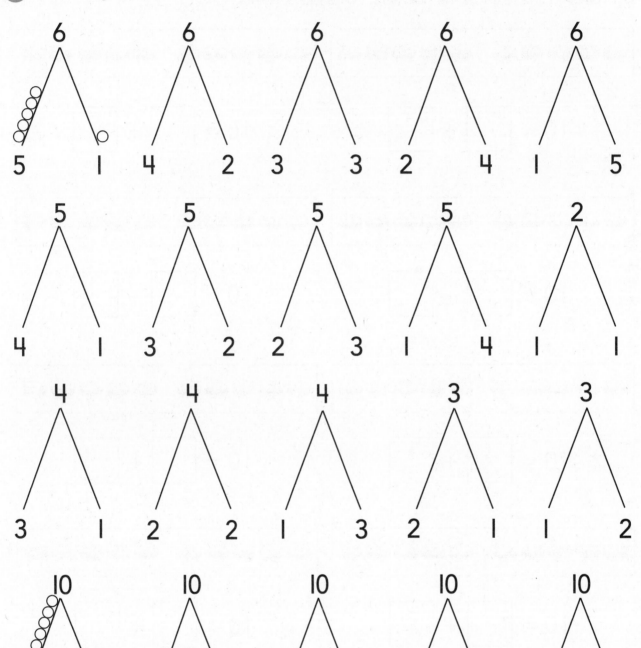

✓ **Check Understanding**

TEACHER: Draw as many 10-partners as you can.

Partners of 10 with 5-Groups

Dear Family:

In your child's math program, partners are numbers that go together to make up another number. For example:

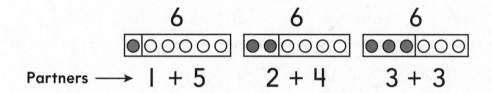

Knowing partners of numbers will help your child develop a strong sense of relationships among numbers and provide a firm foundation for learning addition and subtraction.

Your child has begun using "Math Mountain" drawings to show partners of numbers. Children were told a story about "Tiny Tumblers" who live on top of "Math Mountain." These Tiny Tumblers roll down the sides of Math Mountain for fun. For example:

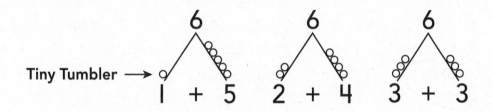

Your child will be asked to count Tiny Tumblers (small circles like those above) and draw Tiny Tumblers to show partners. Children enjoy this visual support and can more easily internalize partners with continued practice. Please help your child with Math Mountain pages as necessary.

Thank you!

Sincerely,
Your child's teacher

Unit 4 addresses the following standards from the Common Core State Standards for Mathematics: **K.CC.A.1, K.CC.A.2, K.CC.A.3, K.CC.B.4, K.CC.B.4.a, K.CC.B.4.b, K.CC.B.4.c, K.CC.B.5, K.CC.C.6, K.CC.C.7, K.OA.A.1, K.OA.A.2, K.OA.A.3, K.OA.A.4, K.OA.A.5, K.NBT.A.1, K.MD.B.3, K.G.A.1, K.G.A.2, K.G.A.3, K.G.B.4, K.G.B.5, K.G.B.6, and all** Mathematical Practices.

Estimada familia:

En el programa de matemáticas de su niño, las partes son números que se juntan para formar otros números, por ejemplo:

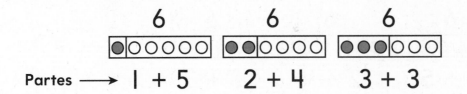

Partes ⟶   1 + 5   2 + 4   3 + 3

Conocer las partes de los números ayudará a su niño a desarrollar la comprensión de las relaciones entre los números y le dará una base firme para el aprendizaje de la suma y la resta.

Su niño ha comenzado a usar los dibujos de "Montañas matemáticas" para mostrar las partes de los números. Los niños escucharon un cuento sobre unas bolitas que viven en la cima de la "Montaña matemática". Para divertirse, las bolitas descienden rodando por el costado de la montaña. Por ejemplo:

Bolitas de la
Montaña matemática ⟶

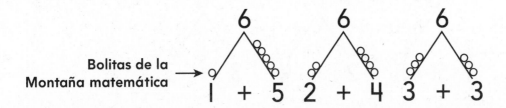

Se le pedirá a su niño que cuente las bolitas y que las dibuje (como se muestra arriba) para mostrar las partes. Los niños disfrutan de este apoyo visual y con la práctica continua pueden asimilar más fácilmente el concepto de partes. Si es necesario, ayude a su niño con las páginas de Montañas matemáticas.

¡Gracias!

Atentamente,
El maestro de su niño

CC SS **En la Unidad 4 se aplican los siguientes estándares de los** Estándares estatales comunes de matemáticas: **K.CC.A.1, K.CC.A.2, K.CC.A.3, K.CC.B.4, K.CC.B.4.a, K.CC.B.4.b, K.CC.B.4.c, K.CC.B.5, K.CC.C.6, K.CC.C.7, K.OA.A.1, K.OA.A.2, K.OA.A.3, K.OA.A.4, K.OA.A.5, K.NBT.A.1, K.MD.B.3, K.G.A.1, K.G.A.2, K.G.A.3, K.G.B.4, K.G.B.5, K.G.B.6 y todos los de** Prácticas matemáticas.

Addition Equations

Name _____

1 Add the numbers.

5 + 1 = ☐   4 + 2 = ☐   3 + 3 = ☐

6 + 1 = ☐   5 + 2 = ☐   4 + 3 = ☐

7 + 1 = ☐   6 + 2 = ☐   5 + 3 = ☐

8 + 1 = ☐   7 + 2 = ☐   6 + 3 = ☐

9 + 1 = ☐   8 + 2 = ☐   7 + 3 = ☐

2 Connect the dots in order.

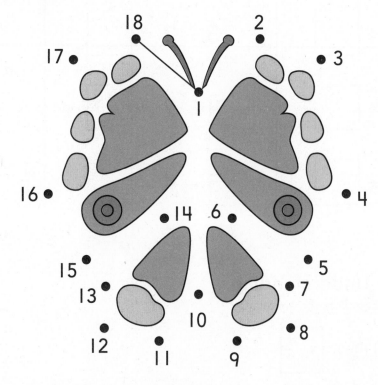

Content Standards K.CC.A.1, K.OA.A.1, K.OA.A.2, K.OA.A.3, K.OA.A.5
Mathematical Practices MP4

3 PATH to FLUENCY **Add the numbers.**

$2 + 3 =$ ⬜ $0 + 2 =$ ⬜ $3 + 1 =$ ⬜

$4 + 0 =$ ⬜ $2 + 1 =$ ⬜ $1 + 1 =$ ⬜

$5 + 0 =$ ⬜ $1 + 2 =$ ⬜ $0 + 3 =$ ⬜

$3 + 2 =$ ⬜ $2 + 2 =$ ⬜ $4 + 1 =$ ⬜

4 PATH to FLUENCY **Subtract the numbers.**

$3 - 2 =$ ⬜ $5 - 5 =$ ⬜ $2 - 2 =$ ⬜

$3 - 3 =$ ⬜ $5 - 2 =$ ⬜ $5 - 1 =$ ⬜

$5 - 0 =$ ⬜ $4 - 2 =$ ⬜ $3 - 0 =$ ⬜

$2 - 1 =$ ⬜ $5 - 4 =$ ⬜ $5 - 3 =$ ⬜

✔ Check Understanding

TEACHER: Complete the equation.

$15 = 10 +$ ⬜

Addition Equations

Name _____

1 Draw Tiny Tumblers on the Math Mountains.

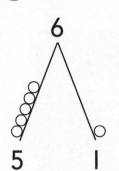
6
5   1

6
4   2

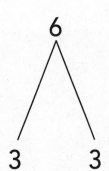
6
3   3

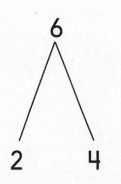
6
2   4

6
1   5

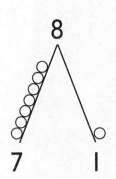
8
7   1

8
6   2

8
5   3

8
4   4

8
3   5

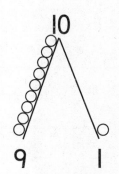
10
9   1

10
8   2

10
7   3

10
6   4

10
5   5

2 Write the numbers 1 through 20.

Content Standards K.CC.A.3, K.CC.B.5, K.OA.A.1, K.OA.A.2, K.OA.A.3, K.OA.A.4
Mathematical Practices MP3, MP6, MP8

Help Kate find the gate.

③ She needs to find the partners of 8.

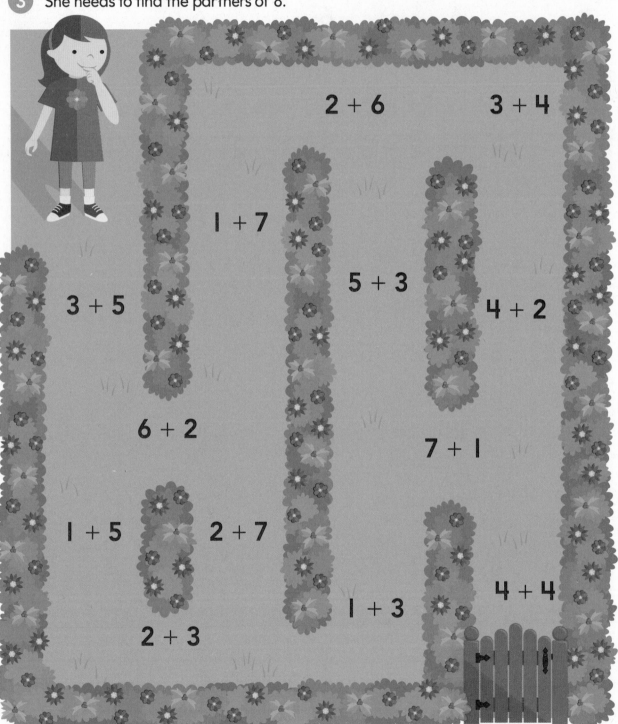

2 + 6   3 + 4

1 + 7

3 + 5   5 + 3   4 + 2

6 + 2

7 + 1

1 + 5   2 + 7

1 + 3   4 + 4

2 + 3

© Houghton Mifflin Harcourt Publishing Company

✓ Check Understanding

TEACHER: Draw objects to show partners for 9. Write the addition expression to match.

More Partners of 10 with 5-Groups

Name _____

VOCABULARY
face
cube

1 Trace around 1 **face** of the **cube**. Use a crayon.

2 Ring each corner.

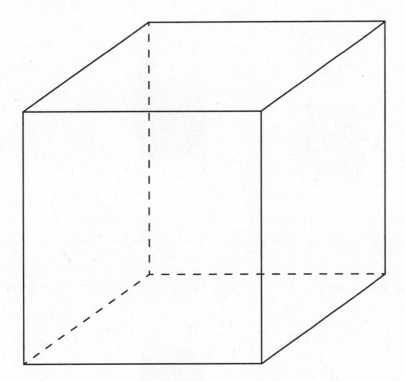

3 How many faces? _____

4 How many corners? _____

5 Look at one face of the cube.
Ring the name of the shape.

square

rectangle

triangle

CC
SS Content Standards **K.G.A.1, K.G.A.2, K.G.B.3, K.G.B.4**
Mathematical Practices **MP1, MP6**

Ring the picture that matches the statement.

VOCABULARY
sphere

6 The cube is below the **sphere**.

7 The cube is in front of the sphere.

8 The cube is above the sphere.

9 The large cube is behind the small cube.

 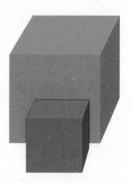

✔ **Check Understanding**

TEACHER: Describe a cube using as many descriptive words as possible.

Identify Cubes

Name _____

1 Add the numbers.

5 + 5 = ☐   6 + 2 = ☐   2 + 7 = ☐

3 + 4 = ☐   4 + 2 = ☐   7 + 3 = ☐

5 + 1 = ☐   4 + 4 = ☐   5 + 4 = ☐

3 + 6 = ☐   5 + 2 = ☐   5 + 3 = ☐

4 + 6 = ☐   3 + 3 = ☐   2 + 5 = ☐

2 Connect the dots in order.

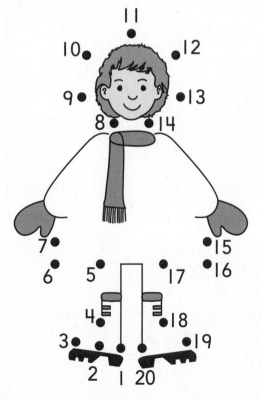

CCSS Content Standards **K.CC.A.1, K.OA.A.1, K.OA.A.2, K.OA.A.5**
Mathematical Practices **MP6, MP7, MP8**

Addition and Subtraction Equations **239**

3 PATH to FLUENCY **Add the numbers.**

4 + 1 = ☐   0 + 3 = ☐   4 + 0 = ☐

3 + 2 = ☐   1 + 4 = ☐   1 + 1 = ☐

5 + 0 = ☐   3 + 1 = ☐   1 + 3 = ☐

2 + 2 = ☐   1 + 2 = ☐   0 + 5 = ☐

4 PATH to FLUENCY **Subtract the numbers.**

5 – 4 = ☐   5 – 2 = ☐   5 – 1 = ☐

4 – 4 = ☐   4 – 2 = ☐   4 – 3 = ☐

3 – 1 = ☐   3 – 0 = ☐   3 – 3 = ☐

2 – 1 = ☐   2 – 2 = ☐   2 – 0 = ☐

 Check Understanding

TEACHER: Add the numbers.

3 + 5 = ☐   6 + 4 = ☐   6 + 3 = ☐

Addition and Subtraction Equations

Name _____   Date _____

1 There are 3 red apples and 6 green apples.
   How many apples in all?
   Draw to show the math story.

_____ apples

2 There are 8 birds on the branch. Then 5 birds fly away.
   How many birds are left?
   Draw to show the math story.

_____ birds

Name _____   Date _____

Use the picture below to complete the questions.

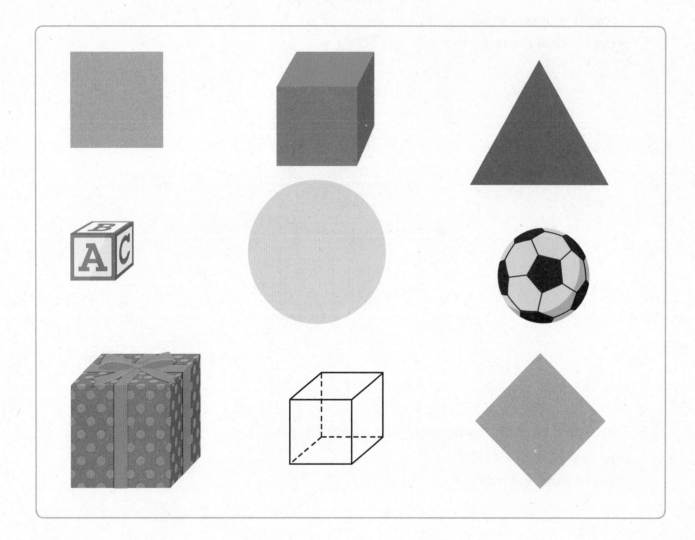

3 How many cubes are there? ☐

4 How many flat shapes are there? ☐

5 How many spheres are there? ☐

6 How many triangles are there? ☐

7 How many solid shapes are there? ☐

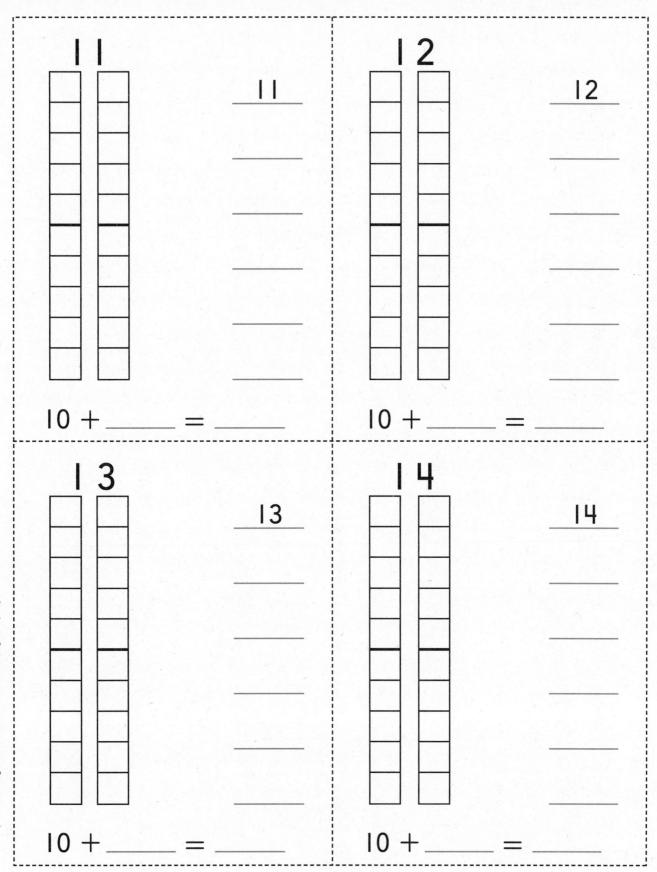

11   11

10 + _____ = _____

12   12

10 + _____ = _____

13   13

10 + _____ = _____

14   14

10 + _____ = _____

Name _____

1 Draw lines to match.

 10

 6

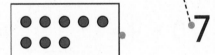 9

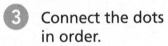 7

 8

2 Draw lines. Make two matches.

 5

 4

 3

 1

 2

3 Connect the dots in order.

5 • • 6

3 • 4 • • 7

9 • • 10

8 •

2 •

1 • • 19

18 • • 17 • 16

15 • 14 • • 13 • 12

• 11

CC SS Content Standards **K.CC.A.1, K.CC.A.2, K.CC.A.3, K.CC.B.5, K.OA.A.1, K.NBT.A.1**
Mathematical Practices **MP2, MP3, MP6, MP7**

4 PATH to FLUENCY **Add the numbers.**

1 + 3 = ☐   3 + 2 = ☐   2 + 1 = ☐

2 + 2 = ☐   1 + 4 = ☐   0 + 2 = ☐

1 + 0 = ☐   1 + 2 = ☐   4 + 1 = ☐

2 + 1 = ☐   2 + 0 = ☐   0 + 4 = ☐

8 + 2 = ☐   2 + 5 = ☐   5 + 3 = ☐

5 + 4 = ☐   6 + 2 = ☐   6 + 4 = ☐

4 + 3 = ☐   2 + 8 = ☐   4 + 3 = ☐

3 + 4 = ☐   5 + 3 = ☐   4 + 5 = ☐

✓ **Check Understanding**

TEACHER: Show the number 13 in different ways: draw groups, draw a 10 stick and extras, write an equation.

Name _____

1 (PATH to FLUENCY) **Add the numbers.**

3 + 1 = ☐

2 + 2 = ☐

0 + 4 = ☐

3 + 2 = ☐

5 + 0 = ☐

4 + 1 = ☐

2 + 0 = ☐

2 + 3 = ☐

0 + 1 = ☐

2 + 1 = ☐

3 + 0 = ☐

1 + 2 = ☐

0 + 5 = ☐

1 + 4 = ☐

1 + 3 = ☐

2 Connect the dots in order.

11
12
•13

10 •   9   8 16 15   •14

7•

•17

2 3 6•
•18

1• •4 •5

20   19

3 (PATH to FLUENCY) Subtract the numbers.

$3 - 2 = \boxed{}$ $5 - 5 = \boxed{}$ $2 - 2 = \boxed{}$

$4 - 1 = \boxed{}$ $4 - 3 = \boxed{}$ $3 - 1 = \boxed{}$

$3 - 3 = \boxed{}$ $5 - 2 = \boxed{}$ $4 - 3 = \boxed{}$

$5 - 0 = \boxed{}$ $4 - 2 = \boxed{}$ $3 - 0 = \boxed{}$

$2 - 1 = \boxed{}$ $5 - 4 = \boxed{}$ $5 - 3 = \boxed{}$

4 Look at what Puzzled Penguin wrote.
Help Puzzled Penguin.

Am I correct?

$4 + 1 = 3$

$4 \quad + \quad 1$ $4 + 1 = \boxed{}$

 Check Understanding
TEACHER: Explain how to solve this equation. $3 + 2 = \boxed{}$

Addition Equations

Name _____

1 Complete the partner equation.

● ● ○ $3 = 2 + 1$

● ○ ○ $3 =$ _____

● ● ● ● ○ $5 = 4 + 1$

● ● ● ○ ○ $5 =$ _____

● ● ○ ○ ○ $5 =$ _____

● ○ ○ ○ ○ $5 =$ _____

● ● ● ● ● ○ $6 = 5 + 1$

● ● ● ● ○ ○ $6 =$ _____

● ● ● ○ ○ ○ $6 =$ _____

● ● ○ ○ ○ ○ $6 =$ _____

● ○ ○ ○ ○ ○ $6 =$ _____

● ● ● ○ $4 = 3 + 1$

● ● ○ ○ $4 =$ _____

● ○ ○ ○ $4 =$ _____

● ● ● ● ● ● ● ● ● ○ $10 = 9 + 1$

● ● ● ● ● ● ● ● ○ ○ $10 =$ _____

● ● ● ● ● ● ● ○ ○ ○ $10 =$ _____

● ● ● ● ● ● ○ ○ ○ ○ $10 =$ _____

● ● ● ● ● ○ ○ ○ ○ ○ $10 =$ _____

● ● ● ● ○ ○ ○ ○ ○ ○ $10 =$ _____

● ● ● ○ ○ ○ ○ ○ ○ ○ $10 =$ _____

● ● ○ ○ ○ ○ ○ ○ ○ ○ $10 =$ _____

● ○ ○ ○ ○ ○ ○ ○ ○ ○ $10 =$ _____

CC SS Content Standards **K.CC.A.2, K.CC.A.3, K.CC.B.5, K.OA.A.1, K.OA.A.2, K.OA.A.3, K.OA.A.4, K.NBT.A.1**
Mathematical Practices **MP2, MP6**

2 PATH to FLUENCY **Add the numbers.**

2 + 2 = ☐   3 + 0 = ☐   2 + 3 = ☐

3 + 1 = ☐   2 + 1 = ☐   1 + 0 = ☐

1 + 2 = ☐   0 + 4 = ☐   3 + 2 = ☐

4 + 1 = ☐   1 + 1 = ☐   0 + 2 = ☐

3 + 4 = ☐   3 + 3 = ☐   5 + 3 = ☐

1 + 5 = ☐   3 + 6 = ☐   8 + 2 = ☐

5 + 2 = ☐   1 + 9 = ☐   5 + 4 = ☐

✔ **Check Understanding**
TEACHER: Complete the partner equation.

8 = _____

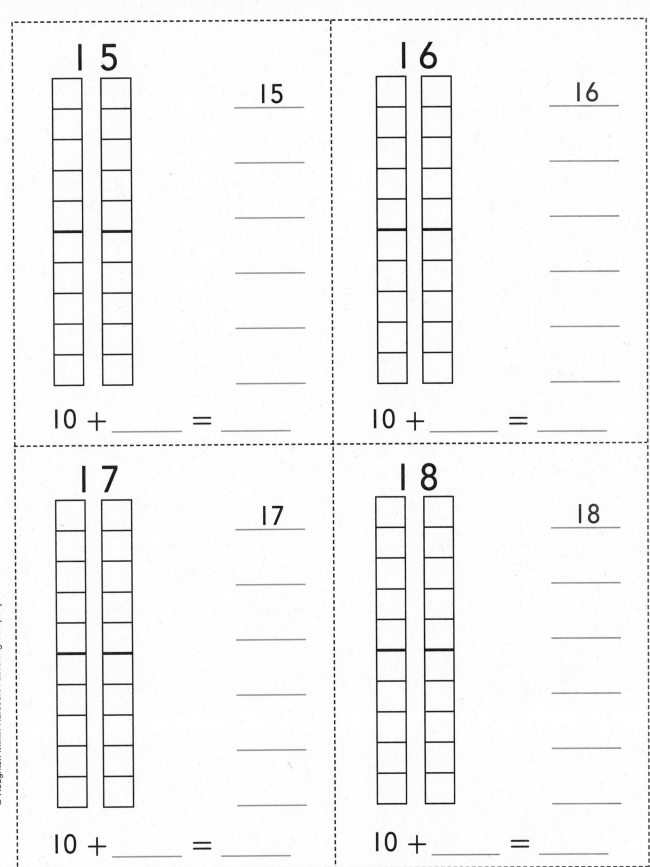

15

10 + _____ = _____

16

10 + _____ = _____

17

10 + _____ = _____

18

10 + _____ = _____

Teen Number Book

1 Write the partner equation.

3 = 1 + 2

_____

5 = 1 + 4

_____

_____

_____

6 = 1 + 5

_____

_____

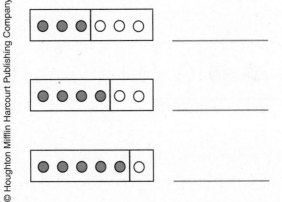

_____

_____

4 = 1 + 3

_____

_____

10 = 1 + 9

_____

_____

_____

_____

_____

_____

_____

CC SS Content Standards **K.CC.A.3, K.CC.B.5, K.OA.A.1, K.OA.A.2, K.OA.A.3, K.OA.A.4**
Mathematical Practices **MP2, MP3, MP6**

Write Addition Equations **253**

2 Subtract the numbers.

$9 - 1 =$ ☐ $8 - 1 =$ ☐ $9 - 5 =$ ☐

$10 - 4 =$ ☐ $9 - 2 =$ ☐ $7 - 2 =$ ☐

$10 - 3 =$ ☐ $8 - 4 =$ ☐ $6 - 1 =$ ☐

$7 - 4 =$ ☐ $6 - 5 =$ ☐ $10 - 2 =$ ☐

$6 - 3 =$ ☐ $6 - 4 =$ ☐ $8 - 2 =$ ☐

3 Look at what Puzzled Penguin wrote.
Help Puzzled Penguin.

$6 = 4 - 2$

Am I correct?

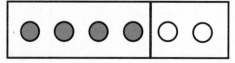

_____

✔ Check Understanding

TEACHER: Explain how you would solve for the partners in this equation.

$10 =$ _____ $+$ _____

© Houghton Mifflin Harcourt Publishing Company

Write Addition Equations

19

19

10 + _____ = _____

20

20

10 + _____ = _____

My

Unit 4

Teen Number

Book

By _____

Fold here.

Teen Number Book

Name _____

1 Draw lines to match.

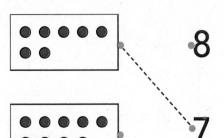 •8

 •7

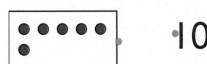 9

 •6

 •10

2 Draw lines. Make two matches.

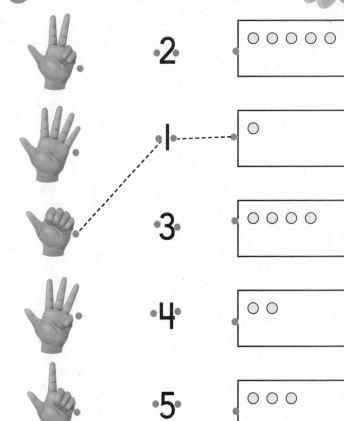

•2

•1

•3

•4

•5

3 Count and write the number. Ring the number that is less.

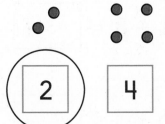

(2) 4

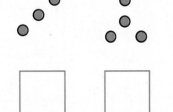

☐ ☐

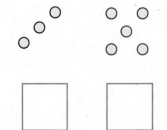

☐ ☐

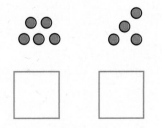

☐ ☐

☐ ☐

Content Standards K.CC.A.2, K.CC.A.3, K.CC.B.4, K.CC.B.5, K.CC.C.6, K.CC.C.7, K.OA.A.1, K.OA.A.2, K.NBT.A.1
Mathematical Practices MP4, MP6, MP7

4 PATH to FLUENCY **Add the numbers.**

$1 + 3 =$ [ ] $3 + 1 =$ [ ] $5 + 0 =$ [ ]

$4 + 0 =$ [ ] $0 + 2 =$ [ ] $2 + 1 =$ [ ]

$1 + 2 =$ [ ] $3 + 2 =$ [ ] $2 + 3 =$ [ ]

$1 + 4 =$ [ ] $2 + 2 =$ [ ] $1 + 1 =$ [ ]

$5 + 3 =$ [ ] $5 + 1 =$ [ ] $8 + 2 =$ [ ]

$2 + 6 =$ [ ] $6 + 4 =$ [ ] $3 + 7 =$ [ ]

$6 + 1 =$ [ ] $4 + 5 =$ [ ] $1 + 8 =$ [ ]

$3 + 7 =$ [ ] $4 + 4 =$ [ ] $6 + 3 =$ [ ]

✓ Check Understanding

TEACHER: Draw to show 19. Use a group of 10 and some ones.

Teen Number Book

Name _____

1 Look at each shape. Write the number of faces.

 ☐

 ☐

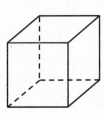 ☐

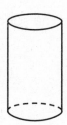 ☐

2 Does the shape **stack** or **roll**? Mark an X.

	Does it stack?	Does it roll?

Use clay and straws to make a cube.

Step 1 Use clay to form 4 spheres as shown.

Step 2 Use 4 straws to connect the spheres of clay.

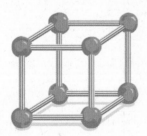

Step 3 Repeat Step 1 and Step 2 to make another square.

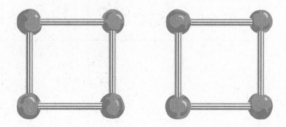

Step 4 Use 4 more straws to connect the squares to form a cube.

✓ **Check Understanding**
TEACHER: Draw an object that is shaped like a cylinder.

Identify Cones and Cylinders

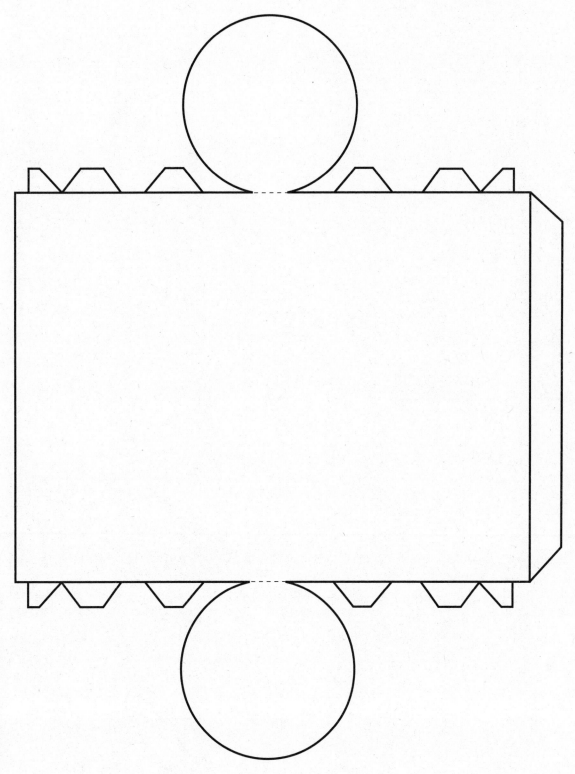

Cylinder Pattern **261**

Cylinder Pattern

Name _____

VOCABULARY
cylinder

1 Ring the objects shaped like cubes on the top shelf.
Ring the objects shaped like **cylinders** on the middle shelf.
Ring the objects shaped like spheres on the bottom shelf.

2 Color each kind of shape.

VOCABULARY
cone

cube   cylinder   **cone**   sphere

Focus on Mathematical Practices

Name _____ Date _____

PATH to FLUENCY

Add the numbers.

1. $2 + 1 = \boxed{}$

2. $1 + 1 = \boxed{}$

3. $1 + 3 = \boxed{}$

4. $3 + 0 = \boxed{}$.

5. $2 + 2 = \boxed{}$

6. $1 + 4 = \boxed{}$

Subtract the numbers.

7. $1 - 1 = \boxed{}$

8. $2 - 2 = \boxed{}$

9. $3 - 0 = \boxed{}$

10. $5 - 2 = \boxed{}$

Name _____ Date _____

Add the numbers.

⑪ 1 + 0 = ☐

⑫ 2 + 1 = ☐

⑬ 2 + 2 = ☐

⑭ 4 + 1 = ☐

Subtract the numbers.

⑮ 2 − 1 = ☐

⑯ 3 − 1 = ☐

⑰ 4 − 0 = ☐

⑱ 3 − 2 = ☐

⑲ 4 − 1 = ☐

⑳ 5 − 4 = ☐

1 Draw a line to show the partners. Write the partners.

$10 = \boxed{} + \boxed{}$

2 The store has 9 apples. Dad buys 3 apples.
How many apples are left in the store?
Draw to show the math story.

_____ apples

3 Which equation shows the partners of 10 for the picture?

○ $10 = 4 + 6$

○ $10 = 7 + 3$

○ $10 = 9 + 1$

④ Subtract. Ring the answer.

5 – 1 = | 4 |
         | 6 |

⑤ Add. Ring the answer.

5 + 0 = | 0 |
         | 5 |

Count and write the number. Ring the number that is less.

⑥

⑦

⑧ Draw lines to match the equation to the drawing.

10 + 4 = 14   10 + 3 = 13   10 + 1 = 11

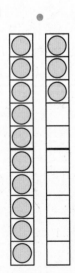   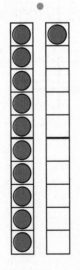   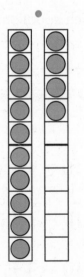

9 Choose all of the solid shapes.

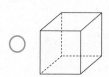 ○    ○   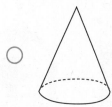 ○   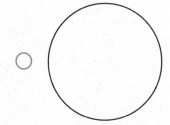 ○

Use the picture below to complete Exercises 10–13.

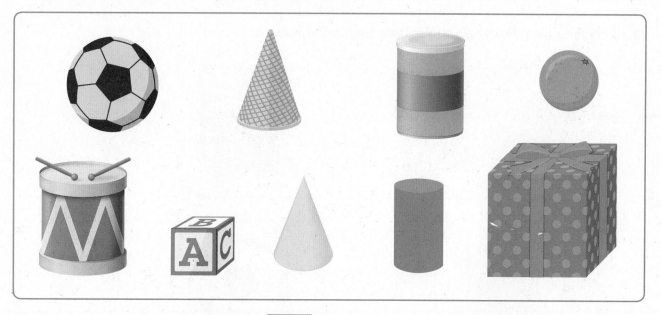

10 How many spheres are there? ☐

11 How many cylinders are there? ☐

12 How many cones are there? ☐

13 How many cubes are there? ☐

14 Ring the cylinder that is next to the cube.

15 Ring the tiles that show the sphere below the cube.

16 Draw to show 14 as 10 ones and extra ones. Complete the equation.

10 + ☐ = ☐

Name _____

Grocery Store Fun

Part A

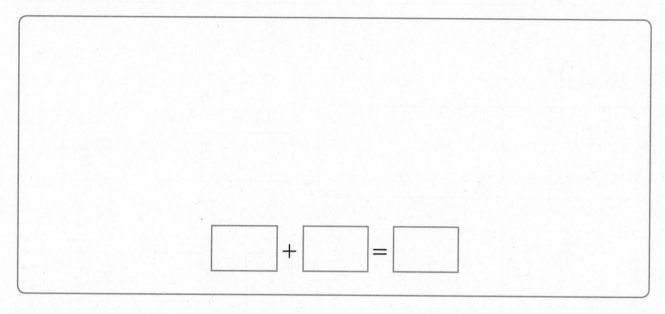

Part B

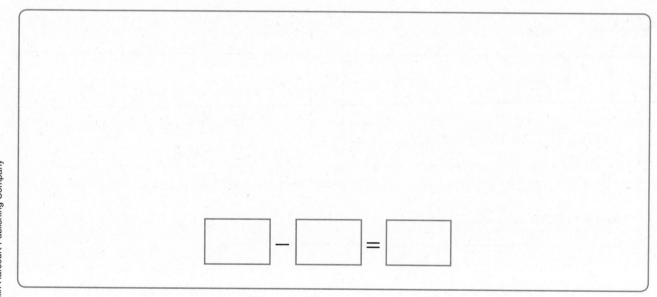

Name _____

Let's Recycle!

Part A

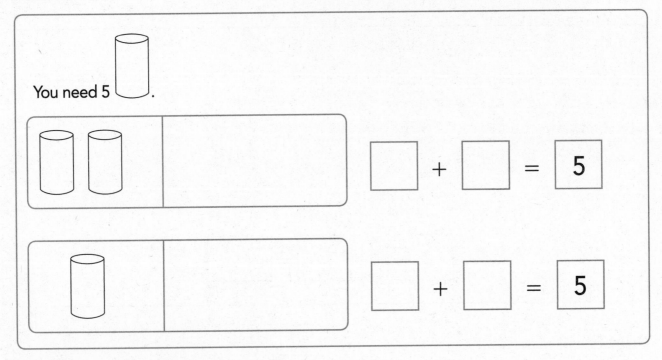

You need 5 ▯.

☐ + ☐ = 5

☐ + ☐ = 5

Part B

You have 7 ▯. You give away _____ ▯.

Now you have _____ ▯.

7 − ☐ = ☐

Dear Family:

We are starting a new unit in math: Consolidation of Concepts. This unit builds on the concepts that were introduced in previous units. For example, children will be creating and solving simple story problems, and making shape pictures. Math projects will include making Teen Number Books and a Night Sky display with stars in groups of ten.

Special emphasis will be on the teen numbers. Here are some ways you can help your child understand teen numbers:

- Make a game of finding teen numbers on signs and in printed materials.

- Encourage your child to count everyday objects (groups of 11–19 items). Ask your child to regroup the objects to show ten ones and extra ones.

- Continue to assist your child with math homework pages.

Thank you!

Sincerely,
Your child's teacher

CC SS Unit 5 addresses the following standards from the Common Core State Standards for Mathematics: **K.CC.A.1, K.CC.A.2, K.CC.A.3, K.CC.B.4, K.CC.B.4.a, K.CC.B.4.b, K.CC.B.4.c, K.CC.B.5, K.CC.C.6, K.CC.C.7, K.OA.A.1, K.OA.A.2, K.OA.A.3, K.OA.A.4, K.OA.A.5, K.NBT.A.1, K.MD.A.1, K.MD.A.2, and all** Mathematical Practices.

Estimada familia:

Vamos a empezar una nueva unidad de matemáticas: Reforzar conceptos. Esta unidad se basa en los conceptos que se han estudiado en las unidades anteriores. Por ejemplo, los niños formularán y resolverán problemas sencillos y harán dibujos de figuras. Los proyectos de matemáticas consistirán en hacer libros de los números de 11 a 19 y un cartel que muestra el cielo de noche con estrellas en grupos de diez.

Se pondrá especial énfasis en los números de 11 a 19. Aquí tiene algunas sugerencias para ayudar a su niño a entender estos números:

- Invente un juego para buscar números de 11 a 19 en letreros y en materiales impresos.

- Anime a su niño a contar objetos cotidianos (grupos de 11 a 19 objetos). Pídale que reagrupe los objetos para mostrar, en cada caso, un grupo de diez unidades y otro grupo con las unidades que sobren.

- Siga ayudando a su niño con la tarea de matemáticas.

¡Gracias!

Atentamente,
El maestro de su niño

En la Unidad 5 se aplican los siguientes estándares de los Estándares estatales comunes de matemáticas: **K.CC.A.1, K.CC.A.2, K.CC.A.3, K.CC.B.4, K.CC.B.4.a, K.CC.B.4.b, K.CC.B.4.c, K.CC.B.5, K.CC.C.6, K.CC.C.7, K.OA.A.1, K.OA.A.2, K.OA.A.3, K.OA.A.4, K.OA.A.5, K.NBT.A.1, K.MD.A.1, K.MD.A.2 y todos los de** Prácticas matemáticas.

capacity

heavier

column

height

decade
numbers

length

heavier

MILK

Capacity is the amount a container can hold.

Height is how tall a person or an object is.

1	11	21	31	41	51	61	71	81	91
2	12	22	32	42	52	62	72	82	92
3	13	23	33	43	53	63	73	83	93
4	14	24	34	44	54	64	74	84	94
5	15	25	35	45	55	65	75	85	95
6	16	26	36	46	56	66	76	86	96
7	17	27	37	47	57	67	77	87	97
8	18	28	38	48	58	68	78	88	98
9	19	29	39	49	59	69	79	89	99
10	20	30	40	50	60	70	80	90	100

The **length** of this pencil is 6 paper clips.

10, 20, 30, 40, 50, 60, 70, 80, 90

lighter	ones
longer	row
one hundred	shorter (height)

18 has 8 **ones**.

lighter

1	11	21	31	41	51	61	71	81	91
2	12	22	32	42	52	62	72	82	92
3	13	23	33	43	53	63	73	83	93
4	14	24	34	44	54	64	74	84	94
5	15	25	35	45	55	65	75	85	95
6	16	26	36	46	56	66	76	86	96
7	17	27	37	47	57	67	77	87	97
8	18	28	38	48	58	68	78	88	98
9	19	29	39	49	59	69	79	89	99
10	20	30	40	50	60	70	80	90	100

longer

The pencil is **longer** than the crayon.

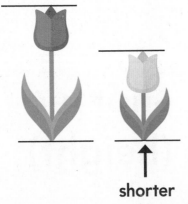

shorter

The yellow flower is **shorter** than the red flower.

1	2	3	4	5	6	7	8	9	10
11	12	13	14	15	16	17	18	19	20
21	22	23	24	25	26	27	28	29	30
31	32	33	34	35	36	37	38	39	40
41	42	43	44	45	46	47	48	49	50
51	52	53	54	55	56	57	58	59	60
61	62	63	64	65	66	67	68	69	70
71	72	73	74	75	76	77	78	79	80
81	82	83	84	85	86	87	88	89	90
91	92	93	94	95	96	97	98	99	100

shorter
(length)

taller

weight

The crayon is **shorter**
than the pencil.

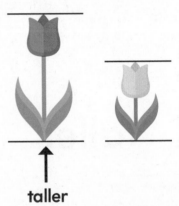

taller

The red flower is **taller** than the
yellow flower.

Weight is how heavy an
object is.

Name _____

1 Draw a row of 10 objects.
Then draw a row with some more objects.
Complete the equation.

$$10 + \boxed{} = \boxed{}$$

2 Draw circles to show a teen number.
Draw squares to show another teen number.
Ring the group with more.
Draw a line under the group with fewer.

✓ **Check Understanding**
TEACHER: Draw a group of objects to show 14 as a group of ten and some extra ones.

Math Stories and Scenes with Teen Numbers

Stars

Name _____

Count the stars. Write the number.

My Count	My Count	My Count

My Count	My Count	My Count

Content Standards K.CC.A.3, K.CC.A.4, K.CC.B.4.a, K.CC.A.4.b K.CC.B.5, K.NBT.A.1
Mathematical Practices MP1, MP3, MP6

Partners of 10: Stars in the Night Sky **279**

Help Puzzled Penguin.

Puzzled Penguin was asked to write three teen numbers.

Did Puzzled Penguin write the numbers correctly?

Did I make
a mistake?

How can we help Puzzled Penguin write the correct numbers?

Write the correct numbers for Puzzled Penguin.

_____   _____   _____

✔ **Check Understanding**
TEACHER: Draw a group of 16 objects.

Partners of 10: Stars in the Night Sky

Dear Family:

It is important that your child learn to see the ten in teen numbers. Each teen number (11, 12, 13, 14, 15, 16, 17, 18, and 19) is made of ten ones and some "extra ones."

Please help your child at home with groups of 11–19 objects. Ask your child to show the group of ten ones, show the extra ones, and then write the number. Below are two ways to display 17 pieces of cereal in a group of ten and extra ones, shown with a sample dialogue about the cereal.

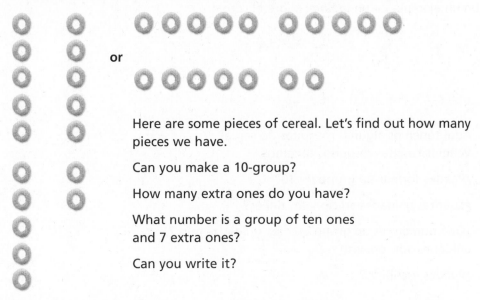

Here are some pieces of cereal. Let's find out how many pieces we have.

Can you make a 10-group?

How many extra ones do you have?

What number is a group of ten ones and 7 extra ones?

Can you write it?

If you have any questions or problems, please contact me. Thank you for your cooperation.

Sincerely,
Your child's teacher

CC SS Unit 5 addresses the following standards from the Common Core State Standards for Mathematics: **K.CC.A.1, K.CC.A.2, K.CC.A.3, K.CC.B.4, K.CC.B.4.a, K.CC.B.4.b, K.CC.B.4.c, K.CC.B.5, K.CC.C.6, K.CC.C.7, K.OA.A.1, K.OA.A.2, K.OA.A.3, K.OA.A.4, K.OA.A.5, K.NBT.A.1, K.MD.A.1, K.MD.A.2,** and all Mathematical Practices.

Estimada familia:

Es importante que su niño aprenda a ver las decenas en los números de 11 a 19. Cada uno de estos números (11, 12, 13, 14, 15, 16, 17, 18 y 19) está formado por diez unidades más algunas "unidades adicionales".

Por favor, ayude a su niño en casa a formar grupos que tengan de 11 a 19 objetos. Pídale que muestre el grupo de diez unidades y las unidades adicionales, y que luego escriba el número. Abajo hay dos maneras de mostrar 17 rosquitas de cereal en un grupo de diez más las unidades adicionales, junto con un ejemplo de un diálogo sobre el cereal.

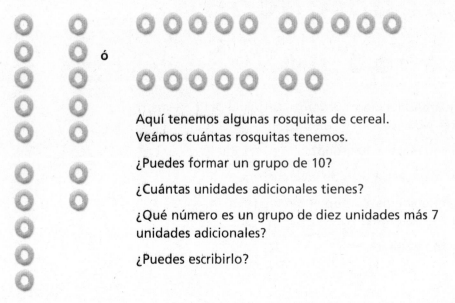

Aquí tenemos algunas rosquitas de cereal.
Veámos cuántas rosquitas tenemos.

¿Puedes formar un grupo de 10?

¿Cuántas unidades adicionales tienes?

¿Qué número es un grupo de diez unidades más 7 unidades adicionales?

¿Puedes escribirlo?

Si tiene alguna duda o pregunta, por favor comuníquese conmigo. Gracias por su cooperación.

Atentamente,
El maestro de su niño

En la Unidad 5 se aplican los siguientes estándares de los Estándares estatales comunes de matemáticas: **K.CC.A.1, K.CC.A.2, K.CC.A.3, K.CC.B.4, K.CC.B.4.a, K.CC.B.4.b, K.CC.B.4.c, K.CC.B.5, K.CC.C.6, K.CC.C.7, K.OA.A.1, K.OA.A.2, K.OA.A.3, K.OA.A.4, K.OA.A.5, K.NBT.A.1, K.MD.A.1, K.MD.A.2, y todos los de** Prácticas matemáticas.

Name _____

Write the equation.

10 = 1 + 9
_____

_____

_____

_____

_____

Content Standards K.CC.A.2, K.CC.A.3, K.CC.B.4, K.CC.B.5, K.OA.A.1, K.OA.A.2, K.OA.A.3, K.OA.A.4, K.NBT.A.1
Mathematical Practices MP3, MP4, MP6

More Partners of 10: Stars in the Night Sky **283**

Draw circles to show each number.
Write the ten and the ones under the circles.
Complete the equations on the bottom.

11	12	13	14	15	16	17	18	19	20
10 + 1	10 +	10 +	+	+	+	+	+	+	+

$14 = 10 + \underline{\hspace{1cm}}$ $17 = 10 + \underline{\hspace{1cm}}$

$15 = 10 + \underline{\hspace{1cm}}$ $19 = 10 + \underline{\hspace{1cm}}$

$12 = 10 + \underline{\hspace{1cm}}$ $16 = 10 + \underline{\hspace{1cm}}$

$13 = 10 + \underline{\hspace{1cm}}$ $18 = 10 + \underline{\hspace{1cm}}$

✓ Check Understanding

TEACHER: Draw a group of ten ones and some extras. Tell your number.

More Partners of 10: Stars in the Night Sky

Name _____

VOCABULARY
ones

Ring the ten ones.
Write the ten ones and more **ones** in each equation.

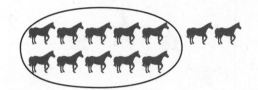

__10__ + __2__ = __12__

_____ + _____ = _____

_____ + _____ = _____

_____ + _____ = _____

_____ + _____ = _____

_____ + _____ = _____

_____ + _____ = _____

_____ + _____ = _____

_____ + _____ = _____

CC SS Content Standards K.CC.A.2, K.CC.A.3, K.CC.B.5, K.OA.A.1, K.OA.A.2, K.NBT.A.1 Mathematical Practices MP1

Solve and Retell Story Problems **285**

Count the stars. Write the number.

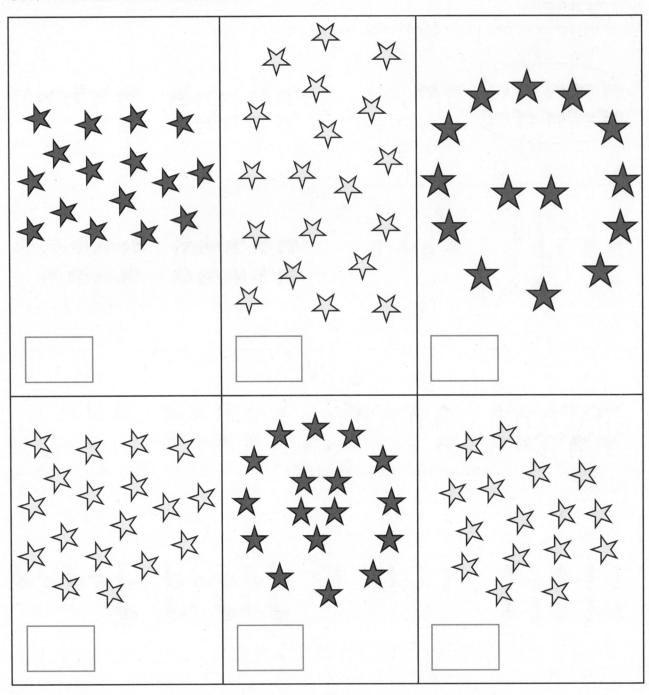

✓ **Check Understanding**

TEACHER: Solve this story problem. There were 3 puppies. Two more come. How many puppies are there now?

_____ puppies

Solve and Retell Story Problems

Fluency Check 4

Name ______________________ Date ____________

PATH to FLUENCY

Add the numbers.

0 + 1 = ☐

1 + 1 = ☐

2 + 2 = ☐

2 + 1 = ☐

1 + 4 = ☐

5 + 0 = ☐

Subtract the numbers.

1 − 1 = ☐

2 − 2 = ☐

4 − 2 = ☐

5 − 3 = ☐

Name _____   Date _____

Add the numbers.

$2 + 0 = \boxed{}$ $1 + 2 = \boxed{}$

$4 + 0 = \boxed{}$ $2 + 3 = \boxed{}$

Subtract the numbers.

$2 - 1 = \boxed{}$ $2 - 0 = \boxed{}$

$3 - 0 = \boxed{}$ $4 - 3 = \boxed{}$

$4 - 4 = \boxed{}$ $5 - 1 = \boxed{}$

Name _____

VOCABULARY
column
row

Write the numbers 1–100 in vertical columns.
Start at the top of each **column** and move down.
Ring the bottom **row** of numbers.
Say these numbers in order to count by tens.

1	11	21							
2									
10									100

Write the numbers 1–100 in horizontal rows.

Ring the last column of numbers.

Say these numbers in order to count by tens.

1	2								10
11									
21									
									100

✔ **Check Understanding**

TEACHER: Explain a pattern you see in the column that starts with 3.

Numbers 1–100

Name _____

There are 6 cows.

There are 3 sheep.

Draw to show how many animals there are.

How many animals are there?

☐ animals

CC SS Content Standards **K.CC.B.5, K.OA.A.1, K.OA.A.2, K.OA.A.3**
Mathematical Practices **MP3, MP4, MP6**

There are 9 ducks.

Then 6 ducks swim away.

Draw to show how many ducks are left.

How many ducks are left?

☐ ducks are left

✓ Check Understanding

TEACHER: There are 6 turtles on a log. Then 3 of them go in the water. How many turtles are left on the log? Make a math drawing to solve the problem, and write the equation.

More Solve and Retell Story Problems

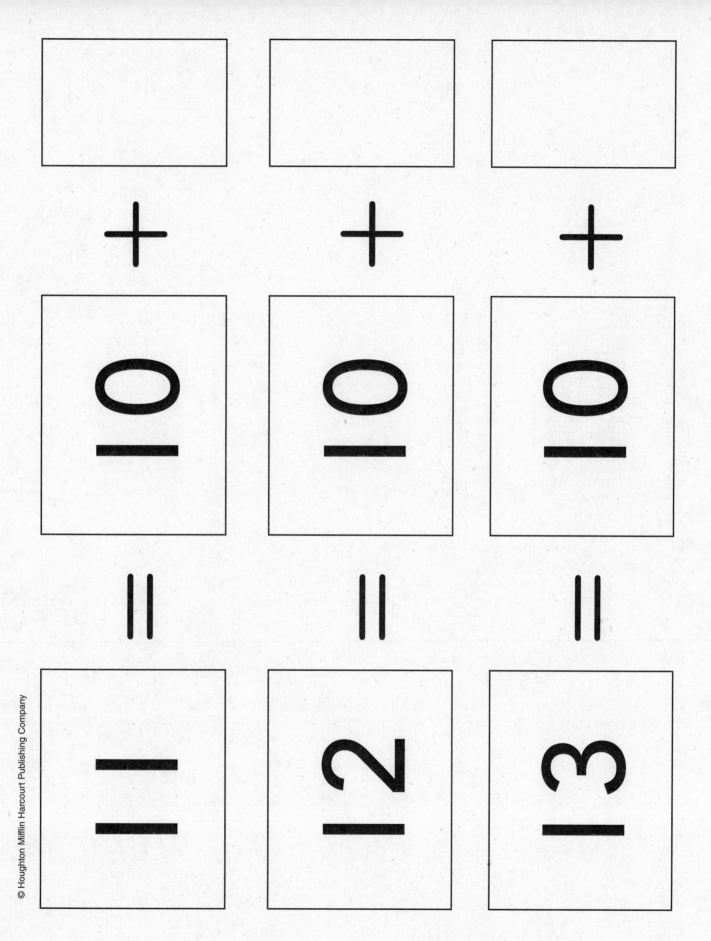

Hiding Zero Gameboard 11–13

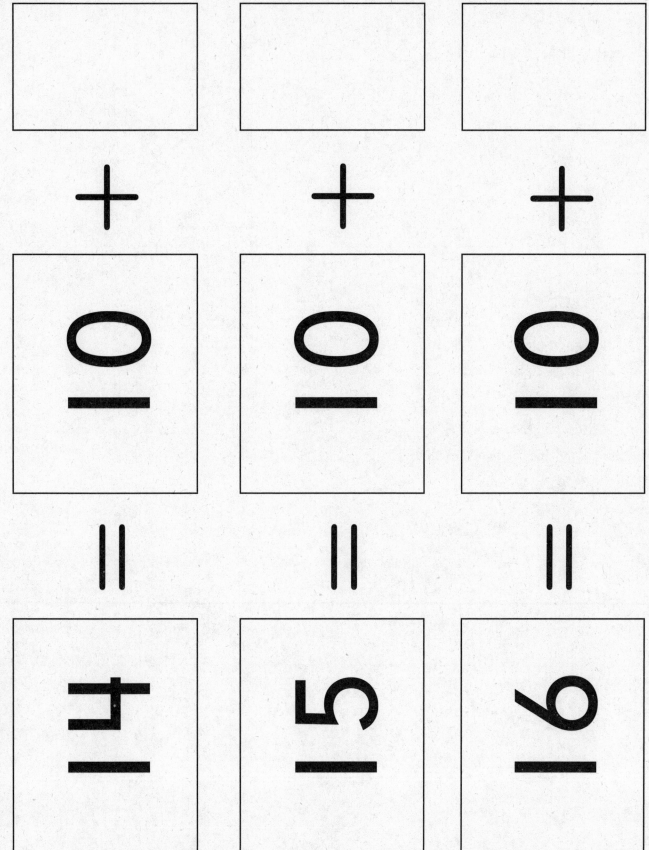

Hiding Zero Gameboard 14–16

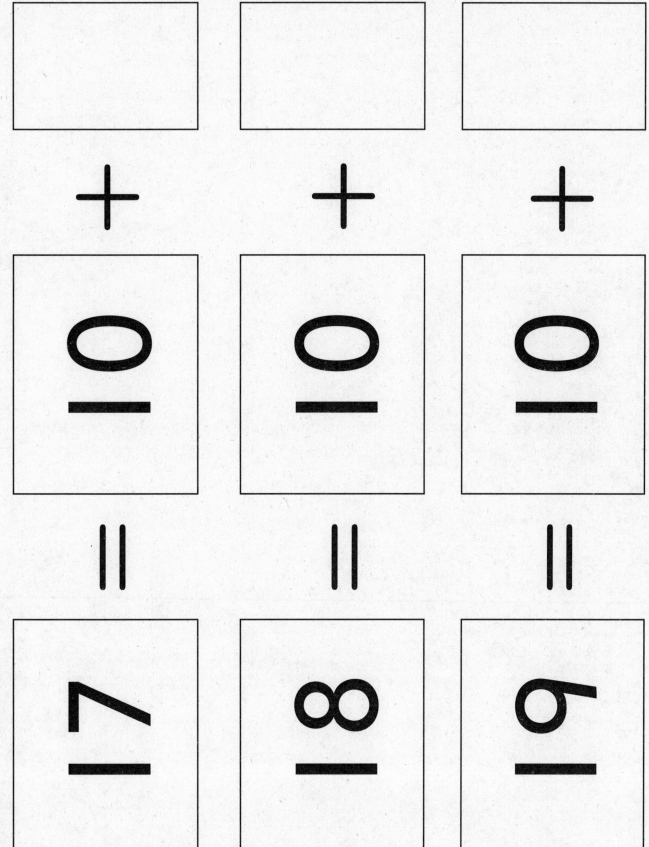

Hiding Zero Gameboard 17–19

Name _____

1 Write the 5-partners. $\boxed{5}$

 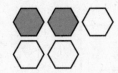 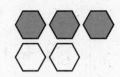 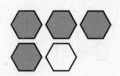

| $1 + 4$ | $2 + 3$ | $3 + 2$ | $4 + 1$ |

   (triangles)

 (diamonds)

  (squares)

Content Standards K.CC.A.3, K.OA.A.1, K.OA.A.2, K.OA.A.3, K.OA.A.5
Mathematical Practices MP6

2 (PATH to FLUENCY) Add the numbers.

2 + 1 = ☐   3 + 1 = ☐   2 + 2 = ☐

2 + 3 = ☐   1 + 3 = ☐   3 + 2 = ☐

5 + 0 = ☐   4 + 1 = ☐   0 + 5 = ☐

3 + 1 = ☐   2 + 2 = ☐   1 + 4 = ☐

3 (PATH to FLUENCY) Subtract the numbers.

5 − 1 = ☐   3 − 2 = ☐   4 − 4 = ☐

4 − 2 = ☐   5 − 3 = ☐   2 − 1 = ☐

5 − 2 = ☐   4 − 3 = ☐   1 − 0 = ☐

4 − 1 = ☐   5 − 2 = ☐   3 − 1 = ☐

✔ **Check Understanding**

TEACHER: Color some circles. Write the partners for 5.

    ◯ ◯ ◯ ◯ ◯ _____

Name _____   Date _____

There are 10 children on the playground.
3 children went home.

1 Use a drawing to show the story problem.

[drawing space]

2 How many children are on the playground now? Write an equation.

_____

There are 13 ducks in a pond.

3 Use counters to show the number of ducks.

4 Write the number of ducks as 10 and some ones.

13 = [ ] + [ ]

Name _____

Draw Tiny Tumblers on each Math Mountain and write the partner.

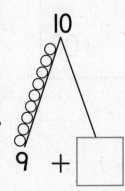 6
5 + 1

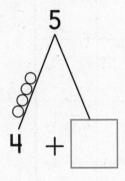 6
4 +

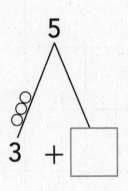 6
3 +

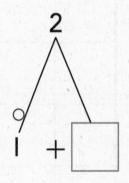 6
2 +

6
1 +

5
4 +

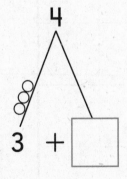 5
3 +

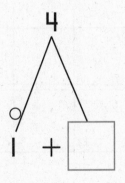 5
2 +

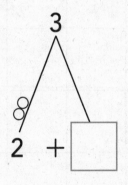 5
1 +

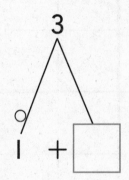 2
1 +

4
3 +

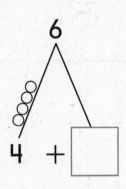 4
2 +

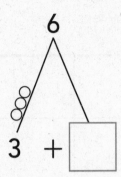 4
1 +

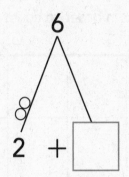 3
2 +

3
1 +

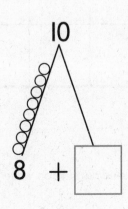 10
9 +

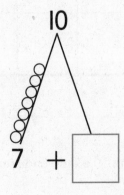 10
8 +

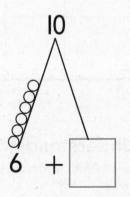 10
7 +

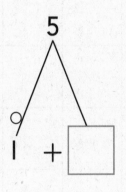 10
6 +

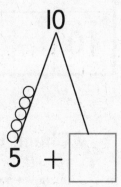 10
5 +

CC SS Content Standards **K.CC.A.1, K.CC.A.2, K.CC.A.3, K.OA.A.1, K.OA.A.3, K.OA.A.4** Mathematical Practices **MP3, MP6**

Write the numbers 1–100.

Ring the bottom row of numbers.

Say these numbers in order to count by tens.

1	11								
2									
10									100

✓ Check Understanding

TEACHER: Draw a Math Mountain with 10 on top and 5 on one side. Then write the unknown partner.

Review Partners

Name _____

1 Write the 6-partners.

⬤〇〇〇〇
〇

⬤⬤〇〇〇
〇

⬤⬤⬤〇〇
〇

⬤⬤⬤⬤〇
〇

⬤⬤⬤⬤⬤
〇

| $1 + 5$ | $2 + 4$ | $3 + 3$ | $4 + 2$ | $5 + 1$ |

_____ _____ _____ _____ _____

⬥
⬥⬥◇
◇◇◇

⬥
⬥⬥◇
◇◇◇

⬥
⬥⬥◇
◇◇◇

⬥
⬥⬥◇
◇◇◇

⬥
⬥⬥◇
◇◇◇

_____ _____ _____ _____ _____

_____ _____ _____ _____ _____

_____ _____ _____ _____ _____

CC SS **Content Standards K.CC.A.3, K.OA.A.1, K.OA.A.2, K.OA.A.3,**
Mathematical Practices MP7

2 PATH to FLUENCY **Add the numbers.**

$1 + 1 = \boxed{}$ $1 + 4 = \boxed{}$ $2 + 1 = \boxed{}$

$1 + 0 = \boxed{}$ $3 + 2 = \boxed{}$ $4 + 1 = \boxed{}$

$2 + 2 = \boxed{}$ $2 + 1 = \boxed{}$ $3 + 0 = \boxed{}$

$2 + 3 = \boxed{}$ $1 + 2 = \boxed{}$ $3 + 1 = \boxed{}$

$1 + 8 = \boxed{}$ $4 + 3 = \boxed{}$ $7 + 3 = \boxed{}$

$6 + 4 = \boxed{}$ $4 + 4 = \boxed{}$ $4 + 2 = \boxed{}$

$5 + 5 = \boxed{}$ $4 + 5 = \boxed{}$ $6 + 2 = \boxed{}$

✔ **Check Understanding**

TEACHER: Solve the equations.

$3 + 3 = \boxed{}$ $5 + 1 = \boxed{}$ $4 + 2 = \boxed{}$

Partners of 6, 7, 8, and 9

Name _____

① PATH to FLUENCY **Subtract the numbers. Use your fingers or draw.**

3 − 2 = ☐   5 − 5 = ☐   2 − 2 = ☐

4 − 1 = ☐   4 − 3 = ☐   3 − 1 = ☐

3 − 3 = ☐   5 − 2 = ☐   4 − 3 = ☐

5 − 0 = ☐   4 − 2 = ☐   3 − 0 = ☐

2 − 1 = ☐   5 − 4 = ☐   5 − 3 = ☐

② **Write the symbol = or ≠ to show equal to or not equal to.**

2 ⊘(≠)   ◯   10 ◯ 2 + 8

5 ◯    ◯ 🖐   6 ◯ 5 + 2

3 ◯   ⚬ ◯ ✊   9 ◯ 3 + 4

1 ◯ • •    ◯   7 ◯ 1 + 6

4 ◯ •••    ◯ 🖐   8 ◯ 4 + 4

3 Count and write how many. Ring the group that has fewer.

| 3 | ⬭2⬭ |

4 Write the numbers from 11 through 30.

✔ **Check Understanding**

TEACHER: Draw two groups of circles. Then use the = sign or ≠ sign to tell whether the groups are equal or not equal.

Tens in Teen Numbers: A Game

10

11

My
Unit 5
Teen Number
Book

By _____

For 10 and 11, draw that many things and circle 10.

Tens in Teen Numbers Book

12

13

14

15

For 12, 13, 14, and 15, draw that many things and circle 10.

Tens in Teen Numbers Book **311**

Tens in Teen Numbers Book

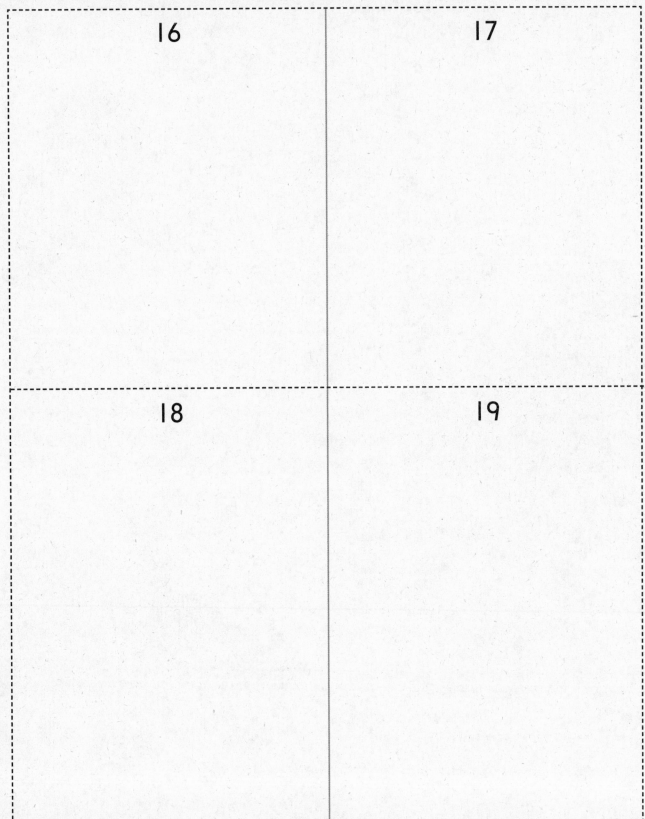

16   17

18   19

For 16, 17, 18, and 19, draw that many things and circle 10.

Tens in Teen Numbers Book

Draw a line to match the 10 partners.

1  •   • 8

2  •   • 6

3  •   • 5

4  •   • 2

5  •   • 9

CC SS Content Standards **K.OA.A.3, K.OA.A.4**
Mathematical Practices **MP6, MP7**

Draw a line to match the 10 partners.

6    •   •   4

7    •   •   3

8    •   •   7

9    •   •   1

✓ **Check Understanding**
TEACHER: Draw objects to show the numbers 14 and 18. Use 10-groups.

       Tens in Teen Numbers Book

Partners of 10

Name _____

Partners of 10

Write the 10-partners in order.

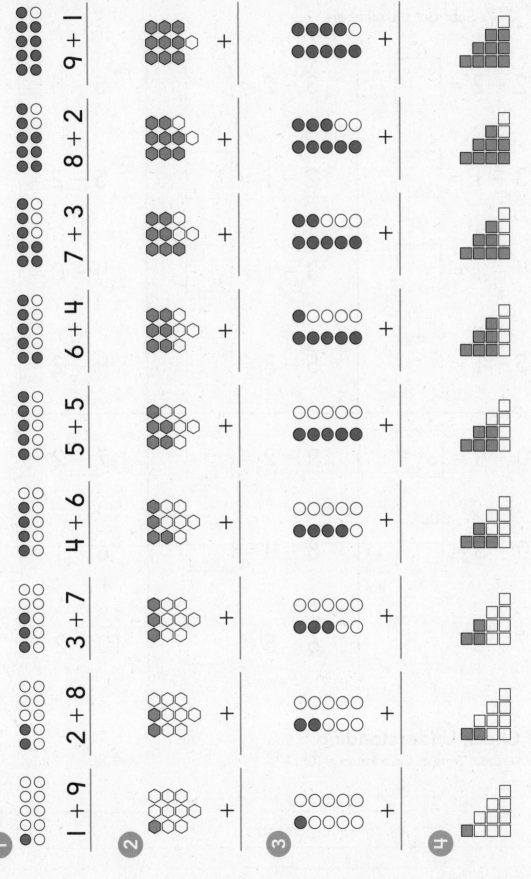

1 9 + 1

2 + 8

3 + 7

4 + 6

5 + 5

6 + 4

7 + 3

8 + 2

1 + 9

5 PATH to FLUENCY **Subtract the numbers.**

2 − 2 = ☐   3 − 2 = ☐   5 − 4 = ☐

3 − 1 = ☐   2 − 1 = ☐   5 − 2 = ☐

4 − 1 = ☐   3 − 1 = ☐   4 − 0 = ☐

5 − 1 = ☐   5 − 3 = ☐   4 − 2 = ☐

10 − 4 = ☐   9 − 2 = ☐   7 − 2 = ☐

10 − 3 = ☐   8 − 4 = ☐   6 − 1 = ☐

7 − 4 = ☐   6 − 5 = ☐   10 − 2 = ☐

 Check Understanding

TEACHER: Write all the partners of 10.

_____

_____

Name _____

Partners of 7
Write the 7-partners in order.

1. 6 + 1
2. 5 + 2
3. 4 + 3
4. 3 + 4
5. 2 + 5
1 + 6

CC SS Content Standards **K.CC.A.3, K.CC.B.4, K.OA.A.1, K.OA.A.2, K.OA.A.3,** Mathematical Practices **MP3, MP4, MP6**

6 Add the numbers.

1 + 2 = ☐   3 + 3 = ☐   8 + 2 = ☐

2 + 5 = ☐   4 + 4 = ☐   7 + 2 = ☐

1 + 6 = ☐   6 + 3 = ☐   6 + 4 = ☐

2 + 8 = ☐   5 + 2 = ☐   5 + 0 = ☐

5 + 3 = ☐   7 + 1 = ☐   2 + 1 = ☐

5 + 4 = ☐   6 + 1 = ☐   4 + 5 = ☐

6 + 2 = ☐   9 + 0 = ☐   7 + 3 = ☐

6 + 0 = ☐   2 + 1 = ☐   8 + 0 = ☐

✓ **Check Understanding**

TEACHER: Explain how you can find all the partners for 7.

Introduction to Counting and Grouping Routines

Name _____

Match. Add shapes to make the two groups equal.
Write the number and the partners.

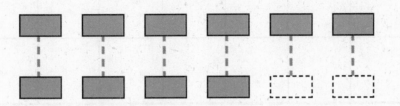

6
_____

4 + 2
_____

_____

_____

_____

_____

_____

_____

_____

_____

© Houghton Mifflin Harcourt Publishing Company

1 Write the numbers 1 through 20.

2 Draw Tiny Tumblers on the Math Mountains. Discuss the way the numbers in the partners change.

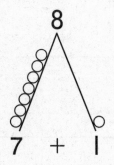
6 + 1

7

5 + 2

7

4 + 3

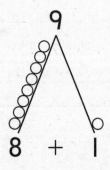
7 + 1

8

6 + 2

8

5 + 3

8

4 + 4

8 + 1

9

7 + 2

9

6 + 3

9

5 + 4

✔ **Check Understanding**
TEACHER: If one partner of 8 is 2, what is the other partner?

Practice: Number Activities

Fluency Check 5

Name ______________________________ Date ______________

PATH to FLUENCY

Add the numbers.

$0 + 0 = \square$

$1 + 0 = \square$

$3 + 0 = \square$

$1 + 1 = \square$

$1 + 3 = \square$

$4 + 1 = \square$

Subtract the numbers.

$1 - 0 = \square$

$4 - 1 = \square$

$3 - 2 = \square$

$5 - 0 = \square$

Fluency Check 5

Name ______________________ Date ______________

PATH to FLUENCY

Add the numbers.

2 + 0 = ☐

0 + 3 = ☐

3 + 2 = ☐

3 + 1 = ☐

Subtract the numbers.

1 − 1 = ☐

2 − 2 = ☐

4 − 2 = ☐

3 − 1 = ☐

4 − 0 = ☐

5 − 2 = ☐

Name _____

Draw Tiny Tumblers. Write how many there are on each Math Mountain.

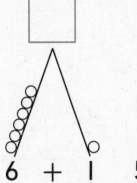

☐   ☐   ☐

6 + 1   5 + 2   4 + 3

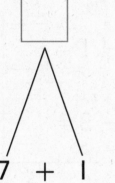   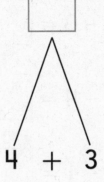

☐   ☐   ☐   ☐

7 + 1   6 + 2   5 + 3   4 + 4

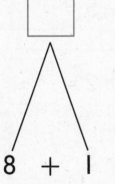  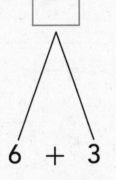  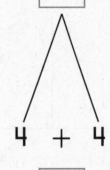

☐   ☐   ☐   ☐

8 + 1   7 + 2   6 + 3   5 + 4

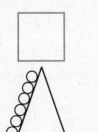 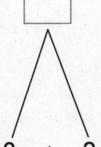   

☐   ☐   ☐   ☐   ☐

9 + 1   8 + 2   7 + 3   6 + 4   5 + 5

CC SS Content Standards **K.CC.A.3, K.CC.B.5, K.OA.A.1, K.OA.A.2, K.OA.A.3, K.OA.A.4** Mathematical Practices **MP2, MP8**

PATH to FLUENCY Subtract the numbers.

5 – 3 = ☐   2 – 0 = ☐   4 – 1 = ☐

3 – 3 = ☐   5 – 4 = ☐   1 – 0 = ☐

4 – 2 = ☐   2 – 1 = ☐   5 – 2 = ☐

5 – 4 = ☐   3 – 2 = ☐   3 – 1 = ☐

4 – 4 = ☐   5 – 1 = ☐   4 – 3 = ☐

9 – 6 = ☐   7 – 2 = ☐   10 – 5 = ☐

7 – 4 = ☐   8 – 6 = ☐   6 – 2 = ☐

10 – 2 = ☐   9 – 5 = ☐   8 – 3 = ☐

10 – 4 = ☐   6 – 3 = ☐   9 – 2 = ☐

✔ **Check Understanding**

TEACHER: Draw Math Mountains to show all the partners of 8. Draw Tiny Tumblers to help.

Add Partners to Find Totals

Name _____

Write the numbers and compare them.

Write G for Greater and L for Less.

Cross out to make the groups equal.

1 ☐☐☐☐☐☐ | 6 | L

☐☐☐☐☐☐☒☒ | 8 | G

2 ●●●●● | ☐ | ___

●●●●●●●●● | ☐ | ___

3 ◺◺◺◺◺◺◺◺◺ | ☐ | ___

◺◺◺◺◺◺ | ☐ | ___

4 ▽▽▽▽▽▽▽ | ☐ | ___

▽▽▽▽▽▽▽▽▽▽ | ☐ | ___

5 ⬭⬭⬭⬭⬭⬭⬭⬭ | ☐ | ___

⬭⬭⬭⬭ | ☐ | ___

6 ♥♥♥♥♥♥♥ | ☐ | ___

♥♥♥♥♥♥ | ☐ | ___

© Houghton Mifflin Harcourt Publishing Company

Puzzled Penguin compared the number of objects in each group, writing G for Greater and L for Less. Cross out the extras to check Puzzled Penguin's answers.

Am I correct?

7
| 6 | L |
| 7 | G |

8
| 8 | G |
| 10 | L |

9
| 9 | G |
| 4 | L |

10
| 7 | L |
| 5 | G |

 Check Understanding

TEACHER: Explain how you compare the number in each group to find which is greater and which is less.

Story Problems and Comparing: Totals Through 10

Name _____

Write the numbers and compare them. Write G for Greater
and L for Less. Add (draw more) to make the groups equal.

1 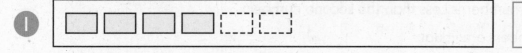 | 4 | L

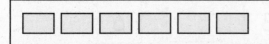 | 6 | G

2  | ☐ | ___

 | ☐ | ___

3  | ☐ | ___

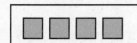 | ☐ | ___

Write the numbers and compare them. Write G for Greater and
L for Less. Subtract (cross out) to make the groups equal.

4  | ☐ | ___

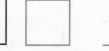 | ☐ | ___

5  | ☐ | ___

 | ☐ | ___

6  | ☐ | ___

 | ☐ | ___

Compare the numbers.

Write G if the first number is Greater than the second number.

Write L if the first number is Less than the second number.

Write E if the numbers are Equal.

4	E	4		8	___	6
7		5		10		1
6	___	9		5	___	5
3		3		6		2
2	___	4		7	___	10

Look at Puzzled Penguin's answers.

Help Puzzled Penguin.

6	L	4
9	G	5
3	L	7
6	G	8

Am I correct?

© Houghton Mifflin Harcourt Publishing Company

✔ **Check Understanding**

TEACHER: Compare the numbers. Write G for greater, L for less, or E for equal.

5 ___ 9   10 ___ 9   8 ___ 8

Subtract to Make Equal Groups

Name _____

Write how many more than ten.
Draw circles to show each teen number.

11 = 10 + __1__

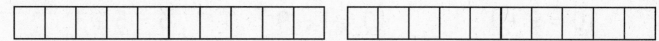

12 = 10 + ____

13 = 10 + ____

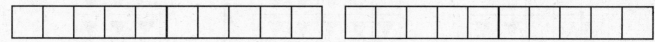

14 = 10 + ____

15 = 10 + ____

16 = 10 + ____

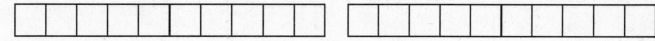

17 = 10 + ____

18 = 10 + ____

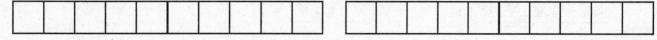

19 = 10 + ____

CC SS Content Standards **K.CC.A.2, K.CC.A.3, K.CC.B.4, K.CC.B.5, K.OA.A.1, K.OA.A.3, K.OA.A.4, K.NBT.A.1**
Mathematical Practices **MP2, MP3, MP6, MP7, MP8**

Tens and Ones **333**

Write the partners.

10

6

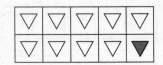

10 = 9 + 1   10 = 1 + 9   6 = 5 + 1

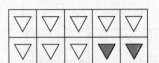

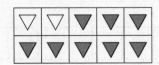

10 = _____   10 = _____   6 = _____

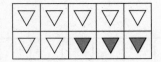

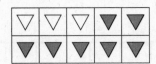

10 = _____   10 = _____   6 = _____

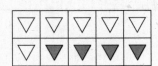

10 = _____   10 = _____   6 = _____

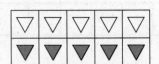

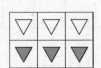

10 = _____   10 = _____   6 = _____

Tens and Ones

Name _____

PATH to FLUENCY Subtract the numbers.

$5 - 3 = \boxed{}$ $4 - 4 = \boxed{}$ $4 - 2 = \boxed{}$

$5 - 4 = \boxed{}$ $5 - 2 = \boxed{}$ $5 - 1 = \boxed{}$

$3 - 1 = \boxed{}$ $3 - 2 = \boxed{}$ $4 - 0 = \boxed{}$

$4 - 3 = \boxed{}$ $2 - 1 = \boxed{}$ $5 - 5 = \boxed{}$

$2 - 2 = \boxed{}$ $4 - 1 = \boxed{}$ $2 - 0 = \boxed{}$

$9 - 1 = \boxed{}$ $8 - 1 = \boxed{}$ $9 - 5 = \boxed{}$

$7 - 2 = \boxed{}$ $10 - 5 = \boxed{}$ $6 - 1 = \boxed{}$

$10 - 1 = \boxed{}$ $9 - 4 = \boxed{}$ $10 - 3 = \boxed{}$

$8 - 4 = \boxed{}$ $6 - 2 = \boxed{}$ $9 - 2 = \boxed{}$

PATH to FLUENCY Subtract the numbers.

$3 - 2 =$ ☐ $\qquad$ $2 - 1 =$ ☐ $\qquad$ $2 - 0 =$ ☐

$1 - 1 =$ ☐ $\qquad$ $3 - 1 =$ ☐ $\qquad$ $4 - 2 =$ ☐

$5 - 4 =$ ☐ $\qquad$ $5 - 0 =$ ☐ $\qquad$ $5 - 3 =$ ☐

$4 - 1 =$ ☐ $\qquad$ $4 - 3 =$ ☐ $\qquad$ $4 - 0 =$ ☐

$5 - 2 =$ ☐ $\qquad$ $4 - 4 =$ ☐ $\qquad$ $5 - 1 =$ ☐

$8 - 5 =$ ☐ $\qquad$ $9 - 3 =$ ☐ $\qquad$ $6 - 4 =$ ☐

$7 - 4 =$ ☐ $\qquad$ $6 - 2 =$ ☐ $\qquad$ $10 - 5 =$ ☐

$10 - 2 =$ ☐ $\qquad$ $7 - 5 =$ ☐ $\qquad$ $9 - 5 =$ ☐

$10 - 3 =$ ☐ $\qquad$ $8 - 4 =$ ☐ $\qquad$ $9 - 2 =$ ☐

✓ Check Understanding

TEACHER: Does switching the order of addition partners change the total? Explain why or why not.

$\qquad$ Tens and Ones

Name _____

Draw circles to show each number.
Write ten and the extra ones under the circles.
Complete the equations on the bottom.

1	2	3	4	5	6	7	8	9	20
1	2	3	4	5	6	7	8	9	

10 + 1   10 +   10 +   +   +   +   +   +   +   +

14 = 10 + ___   12 = 10 + ___   17 = 10 + ___   16 = 10 + ___

15 = 10 + ___   13 = 10 + ___   19 = 10 + ___   18 = 10 + ___

Content Standards K.CC.A.2, K.CC.A.3, K.CC.B.4, K.CC.B.5, K.OA.A.1, K.OA.A.2, K.NBT.A.1 Mathematical Practices MP3, MP5, MP6

Teen Numbers, Partners, and Equations **337**

PATH to FLUENCY Subtract the numbers.

$2 - 1 = \boxed{}$ $5 - 4 = \boxed{}$ $4 - 2 = \boxed{}$

$5 - 3 = \boxed{}$ $4 - 3 = \boxed{}$ $5 - 1 = \boxed{}$

$3 - 0 = \boxed{}$ $3 - 1 = \boxed{}$ $1 - 0 = \boxed{}$

$3 - 2 = \boxed{}$ $3 - 3 = \boxed{}$ $5 - 2 = \boxed{}$

$7 - 4 = \boxed{}$ $9 - 5 = \boxed{}$ $7 - 1 = \boxed{}$

$9 - 2 = \boxed{}$ $10 - 5 = \boxed{}$ $9 - 3 = \boxed{}$

$6 - 4 = \boxed{}$ $8 - 5 = \boxed{}$ $8 - 3 = \boxed{}$

$9 - 1 = \boxed{}$ $8 - 4 = \boxed{}$ $7 - 5 = \boxed{}$

✔ **Check Understanding**
TEACHER: Write the partners for each teen number. Use 10 as one of the partners.

13 _____   16 _____   19 _____

Dear Family:

In the next two lessons, your child will be learning how to compare several measurable attributes of objects, including length, height, and weight. They will also learn how to compare the capacity of containers.

Your child will use the words *longer* and *shorter* to compare the lengths of two objects and the words *taller* and *shorter* to compare heights. You can help your child by practicing these comparisons at home. For example, while having a meal, you might ask your child which is taller, the table or the chair. If your child is drawing, you can ask him or her to compare the lengths of two different crayons. Young children have better success comparing length when the two objects are aligned, as shown here.

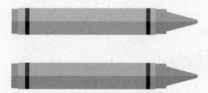

Your child will also be learning to compare weight and capacity. These comparisons may also be practiced at home. You might ask your child to hold a toy in each hand and say which is *heavier* and which is *lighter*. They will be shown that bigger does not always mean heavier. A pillow, for example, may be lighter than a book that is smaller.

Comparisons of capacity can be practiced at mealtime. You might ask your child to say which holds *more* and which holds *less*, the carton of milk or the drinking glass.

Sincerely,
Your child's teacher

CC SS **Unit 5 addresses the following standards from the** Common Core State Standards for Mathematics: **K.CC.A.1, K.CC.A.2, K.CC.A.3, K.CC.B.4, K.CC.B.4.a, K.CC.B.4.b, K.CC.B.4.c, K.CC.B.5, K.CC.C.6, K.CC.C.7, K.OA.A.1, K.OA.A.2, K.OA.A.3, K.OA.A.4, K.OA.A.5, K.NBT.A.1, K.MD.A.1, K.MD.A.2, and all** Mathematical Practices.

Estimada familia:

En las siguientes dos lecciones, su niño aprenderá cómo comparar varios atributos que pueden medirse en los objetos, incluyendo la longitud, la altura y el peso. También aprenderá cómo comparar la capacidad de diferentes recipientes.

Su niño usará los términos *más largo* y *más corto* para comparar la longitud de dos objetos, y los términos *más alto* y *más bajo*, para comparar las alturas. Puede ayudar a su niño practicando estas comparaciones en casa. Por ejemplo, mientras comen, puede preguntarle, cuál es más alta, la mesa o la silla. Si su niño está dibujando, puede pedirle que compare la longitud de dos crayones diferentes. A los niños se les hace más fácil comparar la longitud si los dos objetos que comparan están alineados, como se muestra aquí.

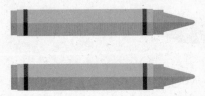

Su niño también aprenderá a comparar peso y capacidad. Estas comparaciones también pueden practicarse en casa. Puede pedirle que sostenga un juguete en cada mano y que diga cuál es *más pesado* y cuál es *más liviano*. Se le enseñará que más grande no siempre quiere decir más pesado. Una almohada, por ejemplo, puede ser más liviana que un libro pequeño.

Las comparaciones de capacidad se pueden practicar a la hora de la comida. Puede pedir a su niño que diga cuál contiene *más* y cuál contiene *menos*, el envase de leche o el vaso.

Atentamente,
El maestro de su niño

En la Unidad 5 se aplican los siguientes estándares de los Estándares estatales comunes de matemáticas: **K.CC.A.1, K.CC.A.2, K.CC.A.3, K.CC.B.4, K.CC.B.4.a, K.CC.B.4.b, K.CC.B.4.c, K.CC.B.5, K.CC.C.6, K.CC.C.7, K.OA.A.1, K.OA.A.2, K.OA.A.3, K.OA.A.4, K.OA.A.5, K.NBT.A.1, K.MD.A.1, K.MD.A.2 y todos los de** Prácticas matemáticas.

Name _____

Write the numbers and compare them. Write G for Greater and
L for Less. Add (draw more) to make the groups equal.

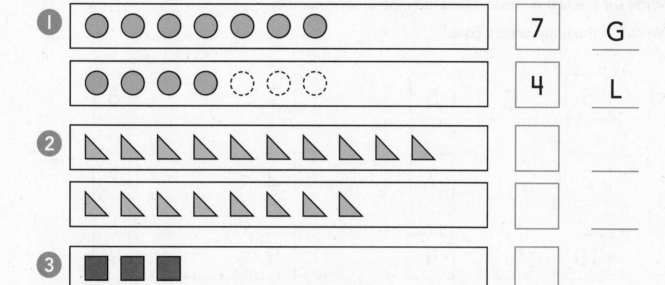

① | 7 | G
| 4 | L

② | |

③ | |

Write the numbers and compare them. Write G for Greater and
L for Less. Subtract (cross out) to make the groups equal.

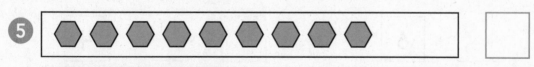

④ | |

⑤ | |

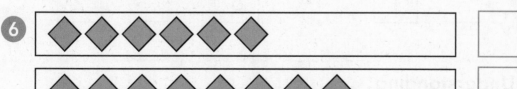

⑥ | |

Compare the numbers.

Write G if the first number is Greater than the second number.

Write L if the first number is Less than the second number.

Write E if the numbers are Equal.

5	E	5		7	___	6
2	___	7		2	___	2
10	___	4		9	___	4
3	___	4		5	___	8
8	___	8		2	___	3
5	___	9		6	___	10
8	___	6		4	___	4
7	___	1		6	___	2

Check Understanding

TEACHER: Draw a group of 7 objects and a group of 5 objects. Add or subtract to make them equal.

More Tens in Teen Numbers: A Game

Name _____

VOCABULARY
longer
shorter (length)

Compare.

Ring the **longer** object.

Draw a line under the **shorter** object.

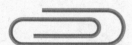

 Draw an object that is longer than this glue stick.

VOCABULARY
shorter (height)
taller

Compare.

Ring the **shorter** object.

Draw a line under the **taller** object.

✓ **Check Understanding**

TEACHER: Ring the correct word.

A cat is _____ than a horse.   shorter   taller

Compare Length and Compare Height

Name _____

Compare.

Ring the object that is **heavier**.

Draw a line under the object that is **lighter**.

Compare.

Ring the object that holds more.

Draw a line under the object that holds less.

 Check Understanding

TEACHER: Complete these sentences to make them true.

A _____ holds more than a paper cup.

_____

A _____ holds less than a sink.

_____

Compare Weight and Compare Capacity

Name _____

Ring the taller animal.
Draw a line under the shorter animal.

1

2

3

4

CC SS Content Standards **K.MD.A.2**
Mathematical Practices **MP3, MP6, MP7**

Ring the longer fish.
Draw a line under the shorter fish.

Focus on Mathematical Practices

Name _____   Date _____

Add the numbers.

$5 + 0 =$ ☐ $0 + 4 =$ ☐

$1 + 2 =$ ☐ $0 + 2 =$ ☐

$1 + 0 =$ ☐ $0 + 0 =$ ☐

$3 + 2 =$ ☐ $0 + 5 =$ ☐

$4 + 1 =$ ☐ $3 + 1 =$ ☐

Name _____ Date _____

Subtract the numbers.

5 − 0 = [　]   5 − 5 = [　]

0 − 0 = [　]   4 − 4 = [　]

2 − 1 = [　]   4 − 3 = [　]

5 − 2 = [　]   4 − 0 = [　]

3 − 1 = [　]   3 − 3 = [　]

Write how many more than ten.
Draw circles to show each teen number.

1 16 = 10 + _____

⬡⬡⬡⬡⬡⬡⬡⬡⬡⬡   ▢▢▢▢▢▢▢▢▢▢

2 17 = 10 + _____

⬡⬡⬡⬡⬡⬡⬡⬡⬡⬡   ▢▢▢▢▢▢▢▢▢▢

3 18 = 10 + _____

⬡⬡⬡⬡⬡⬡⬡⬡⬡⬡   ▢▢▢▢▢▢▢▢▢▢

Ring the ten ones.
Write the ten ones and more ones in each equation.

4

5

_____ + _____ = _____   _____ + _____ = _____

6 Draw a line to match the picture to the partner equation.

 •

• $5 + 4 = 9$

 •

• $2 + 7 = 9$

 •

• $3 + 6 = 9$

 •

• $1 + 8 = 9$

7 Choose the symbol to show equal to or not equal to.

=
≠

4

=
≠

8 Write the numbers and compare them.
Write **G** for **Greater** and **L** for **Less**.
Cross out to make the groups equal.

Draw Tiny Tumblers on the Math Mountain and write the partners. Complete the equation.

9 10

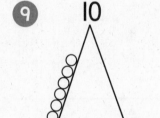

$\boxed{} + \boxed{} = 10$

10 10

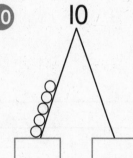

$\boxed{} + \boxed{} = 10$

Use the numbers on the tiles to complete the equations.

6	7	8	9	10

11 $10 - 2 = \boxed{}$ **12** $7 + 2 = \boxed{}$ **13** $4 + 3 = \boxed{}$

14 Ring the heavier object.

---

15 Draw a short baseball bat and a long baseball bat. Ring the longer bat.

---

16 Draw to solve.
There are 5 birds in the field.
Then 2 more birds come to the field.
How many birds are there now?

☐ birds

Name

Star Stories

Name _____

Measures

Part A

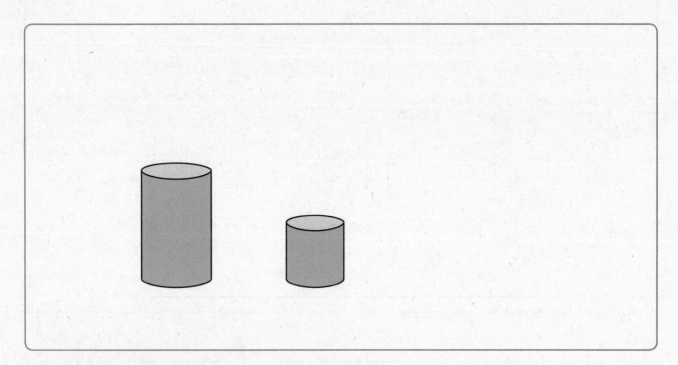

Part B

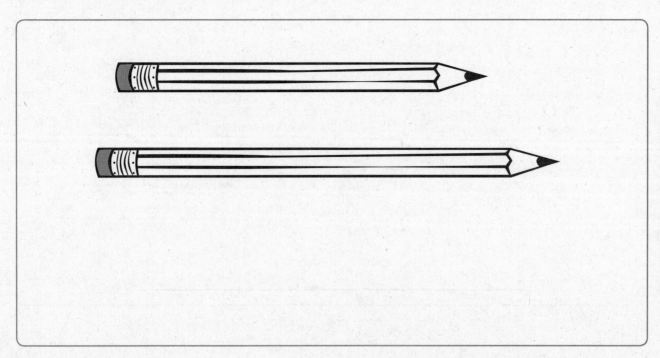

A

above

The bird is **above** the tree.

add

$$3 + 2 = 5$$

B

behind

The boy is **behind** the fence.

below

The tree is **below** the bird.

beside

The slide is **beside** the tree.

C

capacity

MILK

Capacity is the amount a container can hold.

circle

classify

apples

not apples

column

1	11	21	31	41	51	61	71	81	91
2	12	22	32	42	52	62	72	82	92
3	13	23	33	43	53	63	73	83	93
4	14	24	34	44	54	64	74	84	94
5	15	25	35	45	55	65	75	85	95
6	16	26	36	46	56	66	76	86	96
7	17	27	37	47	57	67	77	87	97
8	18	28	38	48	58	68	78	88	98
9	19	29	39	49	59	69	79	89	99
10	20	30	40	50	60	70	80	90	100

cone

corner

corner

count

cube

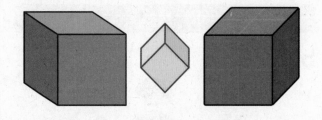

cylinder

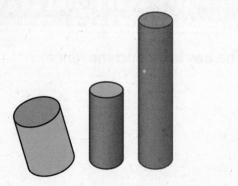

D

decade numbers

10, 20, 30, 40, 50, 60, 70, 80, 90

E

eight

8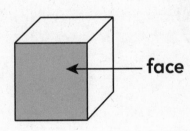

---

equal to sign (=)

4 + 4 = 8

4 plus 4 is **equal to** 8.

---

equation

Examples:

4 + 3 = 7   7 = 4 + 3

9 − 5 = 4   4 = 9 − 5

F

face

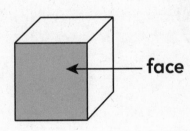

face

fewer

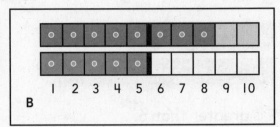

There are **fewer** blue tiles than red tiles.

---

five

5

---

flat shapes

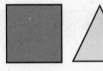

---

four

4

G

greater

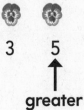

3   5

greater

greater than

6

9

9 is **greater than** 6.

group

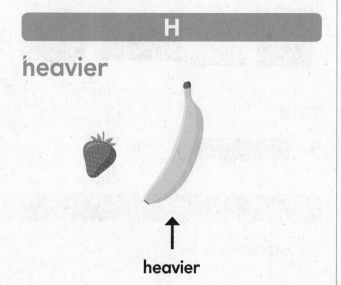

This **group** has 3 circles.

H

heavier

↑
heavier

height

Height is how tall a person or an object is.

hexagon

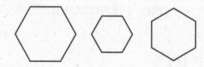

how many

Example:

How many fingers? 5 fingers

2 3 4
1   5

I

in front of

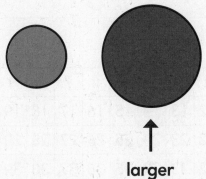

The girl is **in front of** the fence.

L

larger

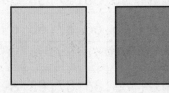

larger

left

The yellow square is on the **left.**

length

The **length** of this pencil is 6 paper clips.

less

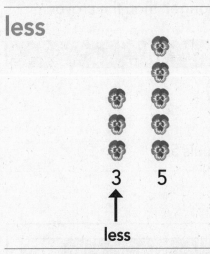

3   5

↑
less

less than

9

11

9 is **less than** 11.

lighter

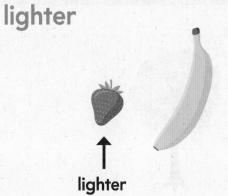

lighter

longer

longer

The pencil is **longer** than the crayon.

M

minus (−)

$8 - 3 = 5$

8 **minus** 3 equals 5.

---

more

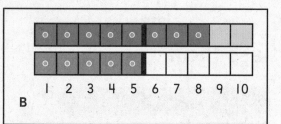

8

5

B

1 2 3 4 5 6 7 8 9 10

There are **more** red tiles than blue tiles.

N

next to

The tree is **next to** the slide.

---

nine

9

---

not equal to sign (≠)

$6 \neq 8$

6 is **not equal to** 8.

O

one

1

---

one hundred

1	2	3	4	5	6	7	8	9	10
11	12	13	14	15	16	17	18	19	20
21	22	23	24	25	26	27	28	29	30
31	32	33	34	35	36	37	38	39	40
41	42	43	44	45	46	47	48	49	50
51	52	53	54	55	56	57	58	59	60
61	62	63	64	65	66	67	68	69	70
71	72	73	74	75	76	77	78	79	80
81	82	83	84	85	86	87	88	89	90
91	92	93	94	95	96	97	98	99	100

ones

18 has 8 **ones.**

order

1	2	3	4	5	6	7	8	9	10

These numbers are in **order.**

P

plus (+)

3 + 2 = 5

3 **plus** 2 equals 5.

R

rectangle

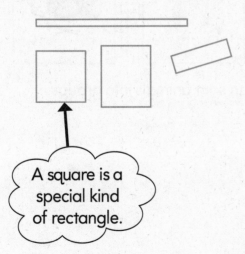

A square is a special kind of rectangle.

right

The green square is on the **right.**

roll

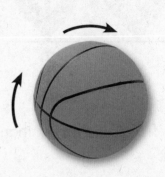

row

1	11	21	31	41	51	61	71	81	91
2	12	22	32	42	52	62	72	82	92
3	13	23	33	43	53	63	73	83	93
4	14	24	34	44	54	64	74	84	94
5	15	25	35	45	55	65	75	85	95
6	16	26	36	46	56	66	76	86	96
7	17	27	37	47	57	67	77	87	97
8	18	28	38	48	58	68	78	88	98
9	19	29	39	49	59	69	79	89	99
10	20	30	40	50	60	70	80	90	100

S

seven

7

shorter (height)

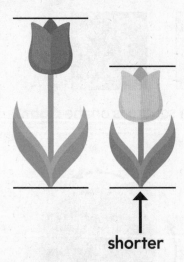

shorter

The yellow flower is **shorter** than the red flower.

shorter (length)

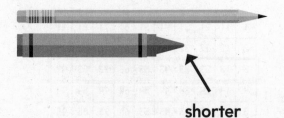

shorter

The crayon is **shorter** than the pencil.

side

side

six

6

smaller

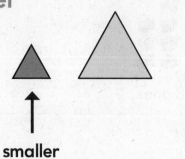

smaller

solid shapes

sort

You can **sort** animals into groups.

sphere

square

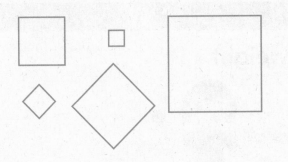

stack

story problem

Example:

There are 2 bunnies in the garden.
Then 3 more bunnies come.
How many bunnies are there in total?

straight lines

Straight lines do not curve.

subtract

$8 - 3 = 5$

⬤⬤⬤⬤⬤ ⬤⬤⬤

T

taller

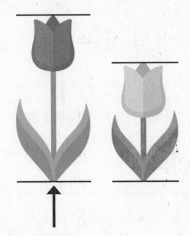

taller

The red flower is **taller** than the yellow flower.

teen numbers

11 12 13 14 15 16 17 18 19

ten

10

three

3

three-dimensional shapes

total

$$4 + 3 = 7$$

↑

total

triangle

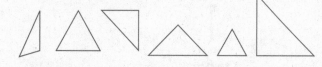

two

2

two-dimensional shapes

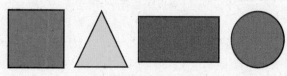

unknown

$3 + 4 = \square$ $3 + \square = 7$

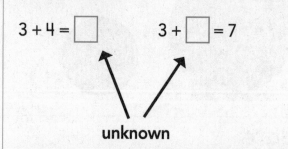

unknown

weight

Weight is how heavy an object is.

zero

0

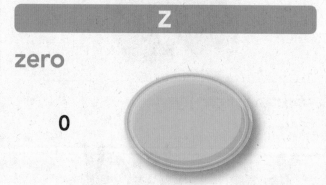

There are **zero** apples on the plate.

K.CC Counting and Cardinality

Know number names and the count sequence.

K.CC.A.1	Count to 100 by ones and by tens.	Unit 1 Lessons 1, 2, 3, 4, 5, 7, 11, 17; Unit 2 Lessons 6, 8, 10, 18, 19; Unit 3 Lessons 1, 2; Unit 4 Lessons 12, 15, 16, 17; Unit 5 Lessons 2, 3, 5, 8, 10, 13, 23
K.CC.A.2	Count forward beginning from a given number within the known sequence (instead of having to begin at 1).	Unit 2 Lessons 1, 9, 10, 14, 18, 19; Unit 3 Lessons 5, 7, 11, 13, 15; Unit 4 Lessons 3, 5, 7, 12, 15, 16, 17, 18, 20; Unit 5 Lessons 3, 4; 5, 7, 8, 9, 10, 15, 18, 19
K.CC.A.3	Write numbers from 0 to 20. Represent a number of objects with a written numeral 0–20 (with 0 representing a count of no objects).	Unit 1 Lessons 6, 12, 13, 14, 16, 17; Unit 2 Lessons 1, 5, 7, 8, 9, 10, 11, 15, 18, 19, 20; Unit 3 Lessons 1, 4, 5, 6, 7, 8, 11, 12, 13, 14, 15, 18, 19, 20; Unit 4 Lessons 1, 2, 3, 4, 5, 8, 10, 11, 16, 18, 19, 20; Unit 5 Lessons 3, 4, 7, 8, 9, 10, 12, 13, 14, 15, 16, 17, 18, 19, 20

Count to tell the number of objects.

K.CC.B.4	Understand the relationship between numbers and quantities; connect counting to cardinality.	Unit 1 Lessons 1, 2, 3, 4, 5, 6, 7, 9, 11, 12, 13, 14, 15, 16, 17; Unit 2 Lessons 1, 2, 3, 4, 5, 7, 8, 9, 10, 11, 15, 16, 19, 20; Unit 3 Lessons 1, 2, 4, 5, 7, 11, 13, 14, 15, 18, 19, 20; Unit 4 Lessons 1, 3, 4, 5, 6, 7, 10, 12, 15, 20; Unit 5 Lessons 2, 3, 7, 9, 13, 14, 15, 16, 17, 18, 19, 23
K.CC.B.4.a	Understand the relationship between numbers and quantities; connect counting to cardinality. • When counting objects, say the number names in the standard order, pairing each object with one and only one number name and each number name with one and only one object.	Unit 1 Lessons 1, 2, 3, 4, 5, 6, 7, 9, 11, 12, 13, 14, 15, 16, 17; Unit 2 Lessons 1, 2, 3, 4, 5, 11, 15; Unit 3 Lesson 2; Unit 4 Lessons 1, 4, 10, 12; Unit 5 Lesson 2

■ **Major**   ■ **Supporting**   ■ **Additional**

K.CC Counting and Cardinality

K.CC.B.4.b	Understand the relationship between numbers and quantities; connect counting to cardinality. • Understand that the last number name said tells the number of objects counted. The number of objects is the same regardless of their arrangement or the order in which they were counted.	Unit 1 Lessons 1, 2, 3, 4, 5, 6, 7, 9, 11, 12, 13, 14, 15, 16, 17; Unit 2 Lessons 1, 2, 3, 4, 5, 7, 8, 11, 15; Unit 3 Lessons 2, 8, 11, 18; Unit 4 Lessons 1, 4, 10, 12; Unit 5 Lesson 2
K.CC.B.4.c	Understand the relationship between numbers and quantities; connect counting to cardinality. • Understand that each successive number name refers to a quantity that is one larger.	Unit 2 Lessons 1, 10, 12, 14, 16, 19, 20; Unit 3 Lessons 11, 12, 13, 14; Unit 4 Lessons 4, 5, 7, 12, 15; Unit 5 Lessons 5, 7, 9, 14, 15, 23
K.CC.B.5	Count to answer "how many?" questions about as many as 20 things arranged in a line, a rectangular array, or a circle, or as many as 10 things in a scattered configuration; given a number from 1–20, count out that many objects.	Unit 1 Lessons 1, 2, 3, 4, 5, 6, 7, 9, 11, 12, 13, 14, 15, 16, 17; Unit 2 Lessons 1, 2, 3, 4, 5, 7, 8, 9, 12, 13, 14, 15, 16, 17, 19, 20; Unit 3 Lessons 1, 2, 3, 4, 5, 6, 7, 8, 10, 11, 12, 13, 14, 15, 16, 17, 18, 19, 20, 21; Unit 4 Lessons 1, 2, 3, 4, 5, 6, 7, 8, 10, 11, 12, 13, 16, 18, 19, 20; Unit 5 Lessons 2, 3, 4, 5, 6, 7, 8, 9, 10, 11, 14, 15, 16, 17, 18, 19, 20

Compare numbers.

K.CC.C.6	Identify whether the number of objects in one group is greater than, less than, or equal to the number of objects in another group, e.g., by using matching and counting strategies.	Unit 1 Lessons 9, 11, 12, 13, 16, 17; Unit 2 Lessons 7, 9, 13; Unit 3 Lessons 10, 12; Unit 4 Lessons 10, 20; Unit 5 Lessons 1, 10, 14, 16, 17, 20
K.CC.C.7	Compare two numbers between 1 and 10 presented as written numerals.	Unit 1 Lessons 9, 15; Unit 2 Lessons 7, 9; Unit 3 Lessons 12, 14; Unit 4 Lessons 6, 10, 20; Unit 5 Lessons 16, 17, 20

■ Major   ■ Supporting   ■ Additional

K.OA Operations and Algebraic Thinking

Understand addition as putting together and adding to, and understand subtraction as taking apart and taking from.

K.OA.A.1	Represent addition and subtraction with objects, fingers, mental images, drawings, sounds (e.g., claps), acting out situations, verbal explanations, expressions, or equations.	Unit 1 Lessons 7, 8, 9, 11, 12, 13, 14; Unit 2 Lessons 2, 3, 4, 5, 6, 9, 10, 11, 12, 14, 15, 16, 19; Unit 3 Lessons 1, 3, 4, 5, 6, 7, 8, 11, 13, 15, 16, 17, 19, 20; Unit 4 Lessons 1, 2, 3, 4, 5, 6, 7, 8, 10, 11, 12, 13, 15, 16, 17, 18, 19, 20; Unit 5 Lessons 3, 4, 5, 6, 7, 8, 9, 10, 11, 12, 13, 14, 15, 16, 17, 18, 19, 20
K.OA.A.2	Solve addition and subtraction word problems, and add and subtract within 10, e.g., by using objects or drawings to represent the problem.	Unit 1 Lessons 7, 8, 14; Unit 2 Lessons 2, 3, 5, 6, 11, 12, 14, 15, 16; Unit 3 Lessons 1, 3, 4, 7, 11, 16; Unit 4 Lessons 1, 2, 3, 4, 6, 7, 8, 10, 11, 12, 13, 15, 16, 17, 18, 19, 20; Unit 5 Lessons 3, 4, 5, 6, 7, 8, 9, 10, 11, 12, 13, 14, 15, 16, 19
K.OA.A.3	Decompose numbers less than or equal to 10 into pairs in more than one way, e.g., by using objects or drawings, and record each decomposition by a drawing or equation (e.g., $5 = 2 + 3$ and $5 = 4 + 1$).	Unit 2 Lesson 2; Unit 3 Lessons 1, 3, 4, 6, 16, 17, 18; Unit 4 Lessons 2, 3, 4, 5, 7, 8, 11, 12, 13, 18, 19; Unit 5 Lessons 3, 4, 5, 6, 7, 8, 9, 10, 11, 12, 13, 14, 15, 16, 18, 19
K.OA.A.4	For any number from 1 to 9, find the number that makes 10 when added to the given number, e.g. by using objects or drawings, and record the answer with a drawing or equation.	Unit 4 Lessons 2, 4, 8, 11, 13, 18, 19; Unit 5 Lessons 3, 6, 8, 11, 12, 13, 15, 18, 19
K.OA.A.5	Fluently add and subtract within 5.	Unit 3 Lessons 4, 5, 6, 7, 12, 14, 18, 19; Unit 4 Lessons 3, 12, 15, 17; Unit 5 Lessons 7, 10

K.NBT Number and Operations in Base Ten

Work with numbers 11–19 to gain foundations for place value.

K.NBT.A.1	Compose and decompose numbers from 11 to 19 into ten ones and some further ones, e.g., by using objects or drawings, and record each composition or decomposition by a drawing or equation (e.g., 18 = 10 + 8); understand that these numbers are composed of ten ones and one, two, three, four, five, six, seven, eight, or nine ones.	Unit 2 Lesson 10; Unit 3 Lessons 2, 3, 5, 6, 8, 13, 15, 17, 18, 19, 20; Unit 4 Lessons 3, 5, 7, 10, 12, 16, 18, 20; Unit 5 Lessons 1, 2, 3, 4, 5, 6, 7, 9, 10, 11, 15, 17, 18, 19, 20, 23

K.MD Measurement and Data

Describe and compare measurable attributes.

K.MD.A.1	Describe measurable attributes of objects, such as length or weight. Describe several measurable attributes of a single object.	Unit 5 Lessons 21, 22, 23
K.MD.A.2	Directly compare two objects with a measurable attribute in common, to see which object has "more of"/"less of" the attribute, and describe the difference.	Unit 5 Lessons 21, 22, 23

Classify objects and count the number of objects in each category.

K.MD.B.3	Classify objects into given categories; count the numbers of objects in each category and sort the categories by count.	Unit 1 Lesson 10; Unit 2 Lessons 13, 17; Unit 3 Lessons 10, 12, 21; Unit 4 Lessons 1, 9, 22

■ Major   ■ Supporting   ■ Additional

K.G Geometry

Identify and describe shapes (squares, circles, triangles, rectangles, hexagons, cubes, cones, cylinders, and spheres).

K.G.A.1	Describe objects in the environment using names of shapes, and describe the relative positions of these objects using terms such as *above, below, beside, in front of, behind, and next to*.	Unit 1 Lessons 8, 10, 18; Unit 2 Lessons 13, 17, 20; Unit 3 Lessons 10, 12, 21; Unit 4 Lessons 9, 14, 21, 22; Unit 5 Lesson 13
K.G.A.2	Correctly name shapes regardless of their orientations or overall size.	Unit 1 Lessons 8, 10, 18; Unit 2 Lessons 13, 17, 20: Unit 3 Lessons 9, 10, 12, 21; Unit 4 Lessons 9, 14, 21, 22; Unit 5 Lesson 13
K.G.A.3	Identify shapes as two-dimensional (lying in a plane, "flat") or three-dimensional ("solid").	Unit 1 Lessons 8, 10, 18; Unit 2 Lesson 13; Unit 4 Lessons 9, 14, 21

Analyze, compare, create, and compose shapes.

K.G.B.4	Analyze and compare two- and three-dimensional shapes, in different sizes and orientations, using informal language to describe their similarities, differences, parts (e.g., number of sides and vertices/"corners") and other attributes (e.g., having sides of equal length).	Unit 1 Lessons 8, 10, 16, 18; Unit 2 Lessons 13, 17, 20; Unit 3 Lessons 10, 21; Unit 4 Lessons 9, 14, 21, 22
K.G.B.5	Model shapes in the world by building shapes from components (e.g., sticks and clay balls) and drawing shapes.	Unit 1 Lesson 10; Unit 3 Lesson 9; Unit 4 Lessons 9, 21
K.G.B.6	Compose simple shapes to form larger shapes.	Unit 3 Lesson 9; Unit 4 Lesson 21; Unit 5 Lesson 13

MP1 Make sense of problems and persevere in solving them.

Mathematically proficient students start by explaining to themselves the meaning of a problem and looking for entry points to its solution. They analyze givens, constraints, relationships, and goals. They make conjectures about the form and meaning of the solution and plan a solution pathway rather than simply jumping into a solution attempt. They consider analogous problems, and try special cases and simpler forms of the original problem in order to gain insight into its solution. They monitor and evaluate their progress and change course if necessary. Older students might, depending on the context of the problem, transform algebraic expressions or change the viewing window on their graphing calculator to get the information they need. Mathematically proficient students can explain correspondences between equations, verbal descriptions, tables, and graphs or draw diagrams of important features and relationships, graph data, and search for regularity or trends. Younger students might rely on using concrete objects or pictures to help conceptualize and solve a problem. Mathematically proficient students check their answers to problems using a different method, and they continually ask themselves, "Does this make sense?" They can understand the approaches of others to solving complex problems and identify correspondences between different approaches.

Unit 1 Lessons 8, 9, 10, 18
Unit 2 Lessons 1, 2, 3, 5, 6, 8, 10, 13, 15, 17, 20
Unit 3 Lessons 1, 4, 7, 16, 21
Unit 4 Lessons 2, 3, 4, 5, 6, 9, 10, 12, 14, 15, 21, 22
Unit 5 Lessons 1, 2, 4, 5, 10, 15, 16, 21, 22, 23

MP2 Reason abstractly and quantitatively.

Mathematically proficient students make sense of quantities and their relationships in problem situations. They bring two complementary abilities to bear on problems involving quantitative relationships: the ability to *decontextualize*—to abstract a given situation and represent it symbolically and manipulate the representing symbols as if they have a life of their own, without necessarily attending to their referents—and the ability to *contextualize*, to pause as needed during the manipulation process in order to probe into the referents for the symbols involved. Quantitative reasoning entails habits of creating a coherent representation of the problem at hand; considering the units involved; attending to the meaning of quantities, not just how to compute them; and knowing and flexibly using different properties of operations and objects.

Unit 1 Lessons 6, 11, 14, 16, 18
Unit 2 Lessons 2, 9, 20
Unit 3 Lessons 1, 3, 4, 10, 11, 12, 14, 21
Unit 4 Lessons 1, 2, 4, 5, 6, 7, 9, 12, 16, 17, 18, 19, 22
Unit 5 Lessons 7, 15, 17, 18, 20, 23

© Houghton Mifflin Harcourt Publishing Company

Common Core State Standards for Mathematical Practice

MP3 Construct viable arguments and critique the reasoning of others.

Mathematically proficient students understand and use stated assumptions, definitions, and previously established results in constructing arguments. They make conjectures and build a logical progression of statements to explore the truth of their conjectures. They are able to analyze situations by breaking them into cases, and can recognize and use counterexamples. They justify their conclusions, communicate them to others, and respond to the arguments of others. They reason inductively about data, making plausible arguments that take into account the context from which the data arose. Mathematically proficient students are also able to compare the effectiveness of two plausible arguments, distinguish correct logic or reasoning from that which is flawed, and—if there is a flaw in an argument—explain what it is. Elementary students can construct arguments using concrete referents such as objects, drawings, diagrams, and actions. Such arguments can make sense and be correct, even though they are not generalized or made formal until later grades. Later, students learn to determine domains to which an argument applies. Students at all grades can listen or read the arguments of others, decide whether they make sense, and ask useful questions to clarify or improve the arguments.

Unit 1 Lessons 1, 2, 3, 4, 5, 6, 9, 10, 11, 12, 14, 15, 17, 18
Unit 2 Lessons 1, 2, 3, 4, 5, 6, 7, 8, 9, 10, 11, 12, 13, 14, 15, 16, 17, 18, 19, 20
Unit 3 Lessons 1, 2, 3, 4, 5, 6, 7, 8, 9, 10, 11, 12, 13, 14, 15, 16, 17, 18, 19, 20, 21
Unit 4 Lessons 1, 2, 3, 4, 5, 7, 8, 9, 10, 11, 12, 13, 14, 15, 16, 17, 18, 19, 21, 22
Unit 5 Lessons 1, 2, 3, 4, 5, 6, 7, 8, 9, 10, 11, 12, 13, 14, 15, 16, 17, 18, 19, 20, 21, 22, 23

MP4 Model with mathematics.

Mathematically proficient students can apply the mathematics they know to solve problems arising in everyday life, society, and the workplace. In early grades, this might be as simple as writing an addition equation to describe a situation. In middle grades, a student might apply proportional reasoning to plan a school event or analyze a problem in the community. By high school, a student might use geometry to solve a design problem or use a function to describe how one quantity of interest depends on another. Mathematically proficient students who can apply what they know are comfortable making assumptions and approximations to simplify a complicated situation, realizing that these may need revision later. They are able to identify important quantities in a practical situation and map their relationships using such tools as diagrams, two-way tables, graphs, flowcharts and formulas. They can analyze those relationships mathematically to draw conclusions. They routinely interpret their mathematical results in the context of the situation and reflect on whether the results make sense, possibly improving the model if it has not served its purpose.

Unit 1 Lessons 1, 2, 3, 5, 7, 8, 9, 11, 12, 13, 14, 17, 18
Unit 2 Lessons 10, 11, 12, 14, 16, 17, 19, 20
Unit 3 Lessons 1, 4, 7, 21
Unit 4 Lessons 2, 4, 6, 8, 12, 14, 20, 21, 22
Unit 5 Lessons 3, 4, 5, 6, 7, 9, 10, 12, 13, 19, 23

Common Core State Standards for Mathematical Practice

MP5 Use appropriate tools strategically.

Mathematically proficient students consider the available tools when solving a mathematical problem. These tools might include pencil and paper, concrete models, a ruler, a protractor, a calculator, a spreadsheet, a computer algebra system, a statistical package, or dynamic geometry software. Proficient students are sufficiently familiar with tools appropriate for their grade or course to make sound decisions about when each of these tools might be helpful, recognizing both the insight to be gained and their limitations. For example, mathematically proficient high school students analyze graphs of functions and solutions generated using a graphing calculator. They detect possible errors by strategically using estimation and other mathematical knowledge. When making mathematical models, they know that technology can enable them to visualize the results of varying assumptions, explore consequences, and compare predictions with data. Mathematically proficient students at various grade levels are able to identify relevant external mathematical resources, such as digital content located on a website, and use them to pose or solve problems. They are able to use technological tools to explore and deepen their understanding of concepts.

Unit 1 Lessons, 14, 18
Unit 2 Lessons 4, 9, 19, 20
Unit 3 Lessons 5, 8, 9, 13, 20, 21
Unit 4 Lessons 5, 7, 9, 14, 20, 21, 22
Unit 5 Lessons 5, 6, 10, 19, 23

MP6 Attend to precision.

Mathematically proficient students try to communicate precisely to others. They try to use clear definitions in discussion with others and in their own reasoning. They state the meaning of the symbols they choose, including using the equal sign consistently and appropriately. They are careful about specifying units of measure, and labeling axes to clarify the correspondence with quantities in a problem. They calculate accurately and efficiently, express numerical answers with a degree of precision appropriate for the problem context. In the elementary grades, students give carefully formulated explanations to each other. By the time they reach high school they have learned to examine claims and make explicit use of definitions.

Unit 1 Lessons 1, 2, 3, 4, 5, 6, 7, 9, 10, 11, 12, 13, 14, 15, 16, 17, 18
Unit 2 Lessons 1, 2, 3, 4, 5, 6, 7, 8, 9, 10, 11, 12, 13, 14, 15, 16, 17, 18, 19, 20
Unit 3 Lessons 1, 2, 3, 4, 5, 6, 8, 9, 10, 11, 12, 13, 14, 15, 16, 17, 18, 19, 20, 21
Unit 4 Lessons 1, 2, 3, 4, 5, 7, 8, 9, 10, 11, 12, 13, 14, 15, 16, 17, 18, 19, 20. 21, 22
Unit 5 Lessons 1, 2, 3, 4, 5, 6, 7, 8, 9, 10, 11, 12, 13, 14, 15, 16, 17, 18, 19, 20. 21, 22, 23

© Houghton Mifflin Harcourt Publishing Company

MP7 Look for and make use of structure.

Mathematically proficient students look closely to discern a pattern or structure. Young students, for example, might notice that three and seven more is the same amount as seven and three more, or they may sort a collection of shapes according to how many sides the shapes have. Later, students will see 7×8 equals the well remembered $7 \times 5 + 7 \times 3$, in preparation for learning about the distributive property. In the expression $x^2 + 9x + 14$, older students can see the 14 as 2×7 and the 9 as $2 + 7$. They recognize the significance of an existing line in a geometric figure and can use the strategy of drawing an auxiliary line for solving problems. They also can step back for an overview and shift perspective. They can see complicated things, such as some algebraic expressions, as single objects or as being composed of several objects. For example, they can see $5 - 3(x - y)^2$ as 5 minus a positive number times a square and use that to realize that its value cannot be more than 5 for any real numbers x and y.

Unit 1 Lessons 1, 4, 5, 6, 7, 8, 9, 10, 17, 18
Unit 2 Lessons 2, 3, 4, 5, 7, 8, 12, 13, 14, 16, 17, 20
Unit 3 Lessons 2, 3, 5, 6, 7, 8, 9, 10, 11, 15, 16, 17, 21
Unit 4 Lessons 1, 2, 4, 5, 6, 7, 8, 9, 11, 12, 13, 14, 15, 16, 20, 21, 22
Unit 5 Lessons 3, 6, 7, 8, 9, 11, 13, 14, 15, 17, 18, 20, 23

MP8 Look for and express regularity in repeated reasoning.

Mathematically proficient students notice if calculations are repeated, and look both for general methods and for shortcuts. Upper elementary students might notice when dividing 25 by 11 that they are repeating the same calculations over and over again, and conclude they have a repeating decimal. By paying attention to the calculation of slope as they repeatedly check whether points are on the line through (1, 2) with slope 3, middle school students might abstract the equation $(y - 2)/(x - 1) = 3$. Noticing the regularity in the way terms cancel when expanding $(x - 1)(x + 1)$, $(x - 1)(x^2 + x + 1)$, and $(x - 1)(x^3 + x^2 + x + 1)$ might lead them to the general formula for the sum of a geometric series. As they work to solve a problem, mathematically proficient students maintain oversight of the process, while attending to the details. They continually evaluate the reasonableness of their intermediate results.

Unit 1 Lessons 4, 7, 10, 11, 14, 17, 18
Unit 2 Lessons 16, 19, 20
Unit 3 Lessons 4, 5, 6, 7, 8, 9, 10, 12, 13, 14, 15, 17, 18, 19, 20, 21
Unit 4 Lessons 5, 6, 7, 9, 13, 15, 22
Unit 5 Lessons 15, 16, 17, 18, 20, 23

Index

© Houghton Mifflin Harcourt Publishing Company

Index

© Houghton Mifflin Harcourt Publishing Company

N

O

P

© Houghton Mifflin Harcourt Publishing Company

of 7, 137, 174, 176, 179, 218, 220, 321, 322, 325, 327

of 8, 137, 235, 236, 322, 324, 327

of 9, 137, 322, 324, 327

of 10, 137, 201–204, 205, 207–208, 219, 220, 229, 235, 249, 253, 315–319, 322, 327, 334

of 11, 145, 184

of 12, 145, 171, 183

of 13, 145, 171, 183

of 14, 145, 171, 183

of 15, 146, 171, 184

of 16, 146, 183, 184

of 17, 146, 171, 184

of 18, 171, 183, 184

of 19, 183

equations, 249, 253, 283, 334

switched partners, 176, 179, 334

Tiny Tumblers, 220, 230, 235, 303, 324, 327

totals, 327

Performance Task. 57–58, 117–118, 191–192, 271–272, 355–356

Position words. *See* **Shapes.**

Problem Solving, 43–44, 75, 87

Puzzled Penguin, 17, 45, 62, 72, 83, 84, 108, 109, 122, 158, 166, 181, 196, 248, 254, 280, 330, 332

R

Rectangle, 29–32, 51–52, 54, 105, 111–112, 149, 153, 185–186, 225

S

Seven. *See also* **Partners.**
groups of, 65, 67–68, 81, 121
writing, 65, 81, 83

Seventeen
tens in, 313
writing, 180

Shapes. *See also* **Geometry.**
combine, 93–94, 147–150
drawing, 49, 56, 150
flat, 226
position
above, 238
behind, 186, 238
below, 186, 238
beside, 186
in front, 238
next to, 186
size, 23–24, 154
sort by, 31–32, 51, 105, 111–112, 153–154, 159–162, 185, 226

Six. *See also* **Partners.**
groups of, 65–68, 71, 74, 121
writing, 65–67, 73–74, 81, 83, 95, 108

Sixteen
tens in, 313
writing, 180

Sorting, 159–162
by color, 154, 159–160, 196
by shape, 31–32, 51, 105, 111–112, 153, 154, 159–162, 185, 226
by size, 159–160

Sorting Cards, 151–152, 155–156, 159–162

Index

Sphere
describe, 259
identify and name, 226, 242, 259, 263–264

Square, 29–32, 51–52, 105, 111–112, 148–149, 153, 185–186, 225

Square-Inch Tiles, 5–6

Story Problems, 43–44, 75, 87, 195

Strategy Check, 241–242, 301

Subtract
fluency practice, 132, 138, 142, 164, 168, 180, 182, 206, 234, 240, 248, 300, 307, 320, 335–336, 338
fluently within 5, 132, 138, 142, 143, 164, 168, 180, 182, 206, 234, 240, 248, 265–266, 300, 307, 320, 329–330, 335–336, 338, 350

Subtraction
addition and, 43–44, 75, 87
equations, 132, 138, 142, 143, 164, 168, 180, 182, 206, 234, 240, 248, 254, 265–266, 292, 300, 307, 320, 329–330, 335–336, 338, 350
Fluency Check, 210, 224, 265–266, 287–288, 326–327, 350
model
drawings, 301
represent problems, 99–100, 206
story problems, 43–44, 75, 87, 301

Switched Partners, 176, 179, 334

Symbols
+/− Tiles, 63–64, 77–78
=/≠ Tiles, 63, 77–78
equal sign (=), 63, 77, 163, 166–167, 307
minus sign (−), 64, 78
not equal to sign (≠), 64, 78, 163, 167, 307
plus sign (+), 63, 77

T

Teen Equation Cards, 203–204

Teen Number Book, 243–244, 251–252, 255–256, 309–314

Teen Numbers, 138, 144, 168, 180, 181–184, 251, 275–276, 279, 333, 337
partners, 171, 183–184, 205, 283–285
writing, 138, 141, 144, 168, 171, 180, 182

Teen Total Cards, 133–134, 169–170

Ten, 201–202. *See also* **Partners.**
count by, 289–290, 304
groups of, 61, 66–68, 96, 97–98, 126, 285, 333
writing, 66, 71–72, 96, 97–98

Ten-Counter Strips, 123–124

Ten-Groups, 145–146, 171–172, 251, 333, 337

Thirteen
tens in, 311
writing, 141

Three. *See also* **Partners.**
groups of, 3, 7–8, 12–13, 18, 38–39, 40, 46, 48, 121
writing, 38, 40, 50, 55, 80, 81

Three-dimensional shapes. *See* **Geometry.**

Tiny Tumblers, 220, 230, 235, 303, 324, 327

Totals
partners, 327

Trapezoid, 149

Be an Illustrator

Illustrator: Josh Brill

Did you ever try to use shapes to draw animals like the seahorse on the cover?

Over the last 10 years Josh has been using geometric shapes to design his animals. His aim is to keep the animal drawings simple and use color to make them appealing.

Add some color to the seahorse Josh drew. Then try drawing a cat or dog or some other animal using the shapes below.

Shape Toolbox

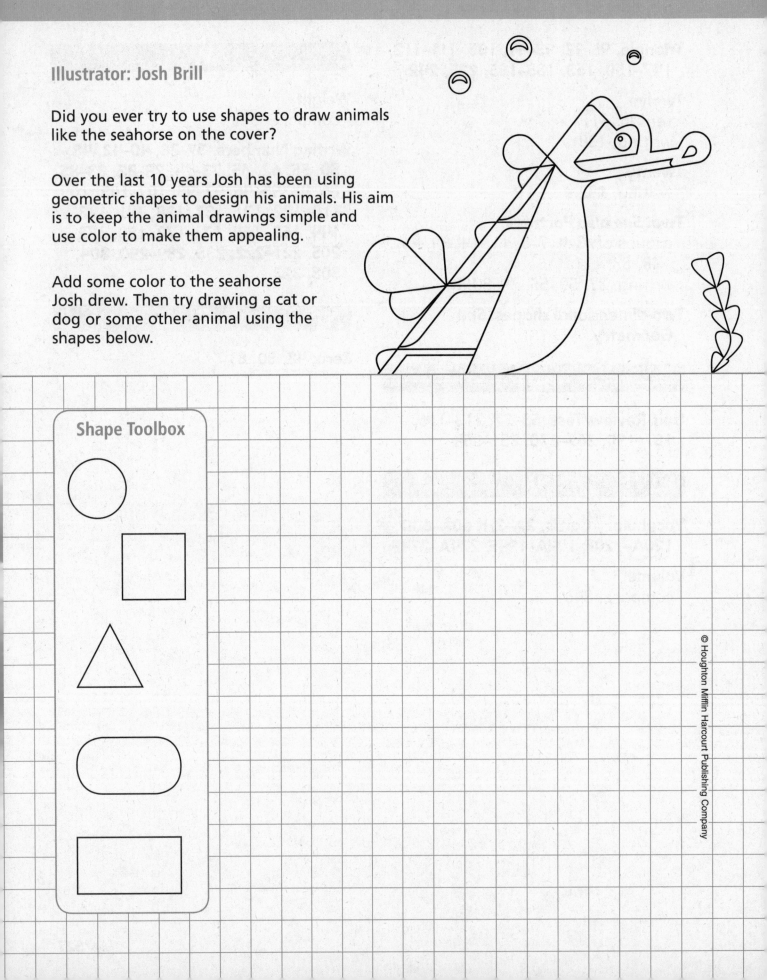